WHAT PEOPLE ARE SA

THE WANDERING ᴠᴠꞮꞮᴜ?

'Gilad Atzmon has written an absorbing and moving account of his journey from hard core Israeli nationalist to a de-Zionized patriot of humanity and passionate advocate of justice for the Palestinian people. It is a transformative story told with unflinching integrity that all (especially Jews) who care about real peace, as well as their own identity, should not only read, but reflect upon and discuss widely.'
Professor Richard Falk, *Albert G. Milbank Professor of International Law Emeritus, Princeton University, author of over 20 books, and UN Special Rapporteur for Occupied Palestinian Territories.*

'Gilad Atzmon has written a fascinating and provocative book on Jewish identity in the modern world. He shows how assimilation and liberalism are making it increasingly difficult for Jews in the Diaspora to maintain a powerful sense of their 'Jewishness.' Panicked Jewish leaders, he argues, have turned to Zionism (blind loyalty to Israel) and scaremongering (the threat of another Holocaust) to keep the tribe united and distinct from the surrounding goyim. As Atzmon's own case demonstrates, this strategy is not working and is causing many Jews great anguish. The Wandering Who? should be widely read by Jews and non-Jews alike.'
John J. Mearsheimer *is the R. Wendell Harrison Distinguished Service Professor of Political Science at the University of Chicago*

'Gilad Atzmon's The Wandering Who? is a series of brilliant illuminations and critical reflections on Jewish ethnocentrism and the hypocrisy of those who speak in the name of universal values and act tribal. Relying on autobiographical and existential experiences, as well as intimate observations of everyday life, both informed by profound psychological insights, Atzmon does what many critics of Israel fail to do; he uncovers the links between Jewish identity politics in the Diaspora with their ardent support for the oppressive policies of the Israeli state.

Atzmon provides deep insights into "neo-ghetto" politics. He has the courage - so profoundly lacking among western intellectuals - to speak truth to the power of highly placed and affluent Zionists who shape the agendas of war and peace in the English-speaking world. With wit and imagination, Atzmon's passionate confrontation with neo-conservative power grabbers and liberal yea sayers sets this book apart for its original understanding of the dangers of closed minds with hands on the levers of power.

This book is more than a "study of Jewish identity politics" insofar as we are dealing with a matrix of power that affects all who cherish self-determination and personal freedom in the face of imperial and colonial dictates.'

Professor James Petras, *Bartle Professor of Sociology at Binghamton University, New York, author of more than 62 books including The Power of Israel in the United States.*

'Gilad Atzmon's book, The Wandering Who? is as witty and thought provoking as its title. But it is also an important book, presenting conclusions about Jews, Jewishness and Judaism which some will find shocking but which are essential to an understanding of Jewish identity politics and the role they play on the world stage.'

Karl Sabbagh *is a journalist, television producer and the author of several books including A Rum Affair, Power Into Art, Dr Riemann's Zeros and Palestine: A Personal History. He is currently the publisher of Hesperus Press*

'Atzmon's insight into the organism created by the Zionist movement is explosive. The Wandering Who? tears the veil off of Israel's apparent civility, its apparent friendship with the United

States, and its expressed solicitude for Western powers, exposing beneath the assassin ready to slay any and all that interfere with its tribal focused ends.'
Professor William A. Cook, *Professor of English at the University of La Verne in southern California, and author of The Rape Of Palestine.*

'The Wandering Who? features Gilad Atzmon at his delightful and insightful best: engaging, provocative and persuasive.'
Jeff Gates, *author of Guilt By Association: How Deception and Self-Deceit Took America to War*

'The Wandering Who? is a pioneering work that deserves to be read and Gilad Atzmon is brave to write this book!'
Dr. Samir Abed-Rabbo, *author and Professor Emeritus in the field of international law. He is director of the Center for Arabic and Islamic Studies in Brattleboro, Vermont and the former Dean of The Jerusalem School for Law and Diplomacy.*

'Gilad Atzmon decided to open Pandora's Box, and ignite a debate that has been frustratingly dormant for too long. His experiences are most authentic, views are hard-hitting, and, at times, provocative. It must be read and discussed.'
Ramzy Baroud, *Palestine Chronicle*

'Gilad's escape from spiritual claustrophobia towards a free and open humanitarianism is fearless. Though his focus here is specific, it seems to me that he offers a potentially liberating suggestion to anyone ready to listen: Isn't culturally exclusive triumphalism a fatally narcissistic dead end?'
Robert Wyatt, *musician.*

'In his inimitable deadpan style, Atzmon identifies the abscess in the Jewish wisdom tooth – exilic tribalism – and pulls it out. Ouch!'
Eric Walberg, *Al Aharam Weekly*

'Having known Gilad for 25 years, I read the book in English, I heard it in Hebrew and reflected on it in Arabic. Gilad Atzmon is astonishingly courageous'

Dr. Makram Khoury, *Senior Lecturer in Media Studies at Anglia Ruskin University, Cambridge, author of Arab Media: From the First Press to New Media*

'Perhaps only a musician could have written this sensitive, perceptive lament over how so many Jews, believing themselves to be doing 'what is good for the Jews,' have managed to carve the heart out of the Palestinian nation and make this tragedy look like the natural order of things.'

Kathleen Christison, *former CIA political analyst and the author of several books on the Palestinian situation.*

The Wandering Who?

A Study of Jewish Identity Politics

The Wandering Who?

A Study of Jewish Identity Politics

Gilad Atzmon

Winchester, UK
Washington, USA

First published by Zero Books, 2011
Zero Books is an imprint of John Hunt Publishing Ltd., Laurel House, Station Approach,
Alresford, Hants, SO24 9JH, UK
office1@o-books.net
www.o-books.com

For distributor details and how to order please visit the 'Ordering' section on our website.

Text copyright: Gilad Atzmon 2011

ISBN: 978 1 84694 875 6

A CIP catalogue record for this book is available from the British Library.

Design: Lee Nash

Printed and bound by CPI Group (UK) Ltd, Croydon, CR0 4YY

We operate a distinctive and ethical publishing philosophy in all
areas of our business, from our global network of authors to
production and worldwide distribution.

CONTENTS

'The Nazis made me afraid to be a Jew, and the Israelis make me ashamed to be a Jew.'

Israel Shahak

Foreword

My grandfather was a charismatic, poetic, veteran Zionist terrorist. A former prominent commander in the right-wing Irgun terror organisation, he had, I must admit, a tremendous influence on me in my early days. He displayed unrelenting hatred toward anything not Jewish. He hated Germans; consequently, he would not allow my dad to buy a German car. He also despised the British for colonising his 'promised land'. I can only assume that he didn't detest the Brits as much as the Germans, however, as he did allow my father to drive an old Vauxhall Viva.

He was also pretty cross with the Palestinians for dwelling on the land he was sure belonged to him and his people. Often, he would wonder: 'These Arabs have so many countries, why do they have to live on the exact same land that was 'given' to us by our God?' More than anything, though, my grandfather hated Jewish leftists. Here it is important to mention that as Jewish leftists have never produced any recognised model of automobile, this specific loathing didn't mature into a conflict of interests between him and my dad.

As a follower of right wing revisionist Zionist Zeev Jabotinsky,[1] my Grandfather obviously realised that Leftist philosophy together with any form of Jewish value system is a contradiction in terms. Being a veteran right-wing terrorist as well a proud Jewish hawk, he knew very well that tribalism can never live in peace with humanism and universalism. Following his mentor Jabotinsky, he believed in the 'Iron Wall' philosophy. Like Jabotinsky, my grandfather respected Arab people, he had high opinions of their culture and religion, yet he believed that Arabs in general, and Palestinians in particular, should be confronted fearlessly and fiercely.

Quoting the anthem of Jabotinsky's political movement my grandpa would often repeat:

From the pit of decay and dust
Through blood and sweat
A race will arise to us,
Proud, generous and fierce.

My Grandfather believed in the revival of the pride of the 'Jewish race', and so did I in my very early days. Like my peers, I didn't see the Palestinians around me. They were undoubtedly there – they fixed my father's car for half the price, they built our houses, they cleaned the mess we left behind, they *schlepped* boxes in the local food store, but they always disappeared just before sunset and appeared again before dawn. We never socialised with them. We didn't really understand who they were and what they stood for. Supremacy was brewed into our souls, we gazed at the world through racist, chauvinistic binoculars. And we felt no shame about it either.

At seventeen, I was getting ready for my compulsory IDF service. Being a well-built teenager fuelled with militant enthusiasm, I was due to join an air force special rescue unit. But then the unexpected happened. On a very late night jazz programme, I heard Bird (Charlie Parker) with Strings.

I was knocked down. The music was more organic, poetic, sentimental and *wilder* than anything I had ever heard before. My father used to listen to Bennie Goodman and Artie Shaw, and those two were entertaining – they could certainly play the clarinet – but Bird was a different story altogether. Here was an intense, libidinal extravaganza of wit and energy. The following morning I skipped school and rushed to Piccadilly Records, Jerusalem's number one music shop. I found the jazz section and bought every bebop recording they had on the shelves, which probably amounted to two albums. On the bus home, I realised that Parker was actually a black man. It didn't take me by complete surprise, but it was kind of a revelation. In my world, it was only Jews who were associated with anything good. Bird was the beginning of a journey.

At the time, my peers and I were convinced that Jews were indeed the Chosen People. My generation was raised on the magical victory of the Six-Day War. We were totally sure of ourselves. As we were secular, we associated every success with our omnipotent qualities. We didn't believe in divine intervention, we believed in ourselves. We believed that our might originated in our resurrected Hebraic souls and flesh. The Palestinians, for their part, served us obediently, and it didn't seem at the time that this situation was ever going to change. They displayed no real signs of collective resistance. The sporadic so-called 'terror' attacks made us feel righteous, and filled us with eagerness for revenge. But somehow, amidst this orgy of omnipotence, and to my great surprise, I came to realise that the people who excited me most were actually a bunch of black Americans – people who had nothing to do with the Zionist miracle or with my own chauvinist, exclusivist tribe.

Two days later I acquired my first saxophone. It's a very easy instrument to get started on – ask Bill Clinton – but learning to play like Bird or Cannonball Adderley seemed an impossible mission. I began to practise day and night, and the more I did, the more I was overwhelmed by the tremendous achievement of that great family of black American musicians I was beginning to know closely. Within a month I learned about Sonny Rollins, Joe Henderson, Hank Mobley, Thelonious Monk, Oscar Peterson and Duke Ellington, and the more I listened the more I realised that my Judeo-centric upbringing was, somehow, totally misleading.

After one month with a saxophone shoved in my mouth, my military combatant's enthusiasm disappeared completely. Instead of flying choppers behind enemy lines, I started to fantasise about living in New York, London or Paris. All I wanted was a chance to listen to the jazz greats play live, for it was the late 1970s and many of them were still around.

Nowadays, youngsters who want to play jazz tend to enrol in a music college. It was very different when I was coming up.

Those who wanted to play classical music would join a conservatory, but those who wanted to play for the sake of the music itself would stay at home and swing around the clock. There was no jazz education in Israel at that time, and my hometown, Jerusalem, had just a single, tiny jazz club, housed in an old, converted picturesque Turkish bath. Every Friday afternoon it ran a jam session, and for my first two years in jazz, these jams were the essence of my life. I stopped everything else. I just practised day and night, even while sleeping, and prepared myself for the next 'Friday Jam'. I listened to the music and transcribed some great solos. I practiced in my sleep imagining the chord changes and flying over them. I decided to dedicate my life to jazz, accepting the fact that, as a white Israeli, my chances of making it to the top were rather slim.

I did not yet realise that my emerging devotion to jazz had overwhelmed my Jewish nationalist tendencies; that it was probably then and there that I left Chosen-ness behind to become an ordinary human being. Years later, I would indeed come to see that jazz had been my escape route.

Within months, though, I began to feel less and less connected to my surrounding reality. I saw myself as part of a far broader and greater family, a family of music lovers, admirable people concerned with beauty and spirit rather than land, mammon and occupation.

However, I still had to join the IDF. Though later generations of young Israeli jazz musicians simply escaped the army and fled to the Mecca of jazz, New York, such an option wasn't available for me, a young lad of Zionist origins in Jerusalem. The possibility didn't even occur to me.

In July 1981 I joined the Israeli army, but from my first day of service I did my very best to avoid the call of duty – not because I was a pacifist, nor did I care that much about the Palestinians. I just preferred to be alone with my saxophone.

In June 1982, when the first Israel–Lebanon war broke, I had been a soldier for a year. It didn't take a genius to figure out the truth. I knew our leaders were lying, in fact, every Israeli soldier understood that this was a war of Israeli aggression. Personally, I no longer felt any attachment to the Zionist cause, Israel or the Jewish people. Dying on the Jewish altar didn't appeal to me anymore. Yet, it still wasn't politics or ethics that moved me, but rather my craving to be alone with my new *Selmer Paris Mark IV* saxophone. Playing scales at the speed of light seemed to me far more important than killing Arabs in the name of Jewish suffering. Thus, instead of becoming a qualified killer I spent every possible effort trying to join one of the military bands. It took a few months, but I eventually landed safely in the Israeli Air Force Orchestra (IAFO).

The IAFO was uniquely constituted. You could be accepted for being an excellent musician or promising talent, or for being a son of a dead pilot. The fact that I was accepted knowing that my dad was still amongst the living reassured me: for the first time, I considered the possibility that I might possess musical talent.

To my great surprise, none of the orchestra members took the army seriously. We were all concerned with just one thing: our personal musical development. We hated the army, and it didn't take long before I began to hate the very state that required an Air Force that required a band for it, that stopped me from practising 24/7. When we were called to play for a military event, we would try and play as poorly as we could just to make sure we would never get invited again. Sometimes we even gathered in the afternoon just to *practise* playing badly. We realised that the worse we performed as a collective, the more personal freedom we would gain. In the military orchestra I learned for the first time how to be subversive, how to sabotage the system in order to strive for a personal ideal.

In the summer of 1984, just three weeks before I shed my military uniform, we were sent to Lebanon for a concert tour. At the time it was a very dangerous place to be. The Israeli army was dug deep in bunkers and trenches, avoiding any confrontations with the local population. On the second day we set out for Ansar, a notorious Israeli internment camp in South Lebanon. This experience was to change my life completely.

At the end of a dusty dirt track, on a boiling hot day in early July, we arrived at hell on earth. The huge detention centre was enclosed with barbed wire. As we drove to the camp headquarters, we had a view of thousands of inmates in the open air being scorched by the sun.

As difficult as it might be to believe, military bands are always treated as VIPs, and once we landed at the officers' barracks we were taken on a guided tour of the camp. We walked along the endless barbed wire and guard towers. I couldn't believe my eyes.

'Who are these people?' I asked the officer.

'Palestinians,' he said. 'On the left are PLO [Palestine Liberation Organisation], and on the right are Ahmed Jibril's boys [Popular Front for the Liberation of Palestine – General Command] – they are far more dangerous, so we keep them isolated.'

I studied the detainees. They looked very different to the Palestinians in Jerusalem. The ones I saw in Ansar were angry. They were not defeated, they were freedom fighters and they were numerous. As we continued past the barbed wire I continued gazing at the inmates, and arrived at an unbearable truth: I was walking on the other side, in Israeli military uniform. The place was a concentration camp. The inmates were the 'Jews', and I was nothing but a 'Nazi'. It took me years to admit to myself that even the binary opposition Jew/Nazi was in itself a result of my Judeo-centric indoctrination.

While I contemplated the resonance of my uniform, trying to deal with the great sense of shame growing in me, we came to a large, flat ground at the centre of the camp. The officer guiding us offered more platitudes about the current war to defend our Jewish haven. While he was boring us to death with these irrelevant *Hasbara* (propaganda) lies, I noticed that we were surrounded by two dozen concrete blocks each around 1m^2 in area and 1.3m high, with small metal doors as entrances. I was horrified at the thought that my army was locking guard dogs into these boxes for the night. Putting my Israeli *chutzpah* into action, I confronted the officer about these horrible concrete dog cubes. He was quick to reply: 'These are our solitary confinement blocks; after two days in one of these, you become a devoted Zionist!'

This was enough for me. I realised that my affair with the Israeli state and with Zionism was over. Yet I still knew very little about Palestine, about the *Nakba* or even about Judaism and Jewish-ness, for that matter. I only saw then that, as far as I was concerned, Israel was bad news, and I didn't want to have anything further to do with it. Two weeks later I returned my uniform, grabbed my alto sax, took the bus to Ben-Gurion Airport and left for Europe for a few months, to busk in the street. At the age of twenty-one, I was free for the first time. However, December proved too cold for me, and I returned home – but with the clear intention to make it back to Europe. I somehow already yearned to become a *Goy* or at least to be surrounded by *Goyim*.

***

It took another ten years before I could leave Israel for good. During that time, however, I began to learn about the Israel–Palestine conflict, and to accept that I was actually living on someone else's land. I took in the devastating fact that in 1948 the Palestinians hadn't abandoned their homes willingly – as we were told in school – but had been brutally ethnically cleansed by my grandfather and his ilk. I began to realise that ethnic

7

cleansing has never stopped in Israel, but has instead just taken on different forms, and to acknowledge the fact that the Israeli legal system was not impartial but racially-orientated (for example, the 'Law of Return' welcomes Jews 'home' from any country supposedly after 2,000 years, but prevents Palestinians from returning to their villages after two years abroad). All the while, I had also been developing as a musician, becoming a major session player and a musical producer. I wasn't really involved in any political activity, and though I scrutinised the Israeli leftist discourse I soon realised that it was largely a social club rather than an ideological force motivated by ethical awareness.

At the time of the Oslo Accords in 1993, I just couldn't take it anymore. I saw that Israeli 'peacemaking' was nothing but spin. Its purpose wasn't to reconcile with the Palestinians or confront Zionist original sin, but to further secure the existence of the Jewish State at the expense of the Palestinians. For most Israelis, *shalom* doesn't mean 'peace', it means security, and for Jews only. For Palestinians to celebrate their 'Right of Return' wasn't an option. I decided to leave my home and my career. I left everything and everyone behind, including my wife Tali, who joined me later. All I took with me was my tenor saxophone – my true, eternal friend.

I moved to London and began postgraduate studies in philosophy at the University of Essex. Within a week, I managed to obtain a residency at the Black Lion, a legendary Irish pub on the Kilburn High Road. At the time I failed to appreciate how lucky I was – I didn't know how difficult it was to get a gig in London. In fact, this was the beginning of my international career as a jazz musician. Within a year I had become very popular in the UK, playing bebop and post-bop. Within three years I was playing with my band all over Europe.

Yet it didn't take long before I began to feel homesick. To my great surprise, it wasn't Israel I missed; not Tel Aviv, not Haifa, not Jerusalem. It was *Palestine*. It wasn't the rude and loud Israeli taxi drivers at Ben-Gurion Airport, or grimy shopping centres in Ramat Gan, but the little place in Yefet Street, Jaffa that served the best hummus money can buy, and the Palestinian villages stretched across the hills amidst olive trees and *sabra* cacti. Whenever I fancied a visit home, in London, I would end up on the Edgware Road, spending the evening at a Lebanese restaurant. Once I started to fully express my thoughts about Israel in public, it soon became clear to me that Edgware Road was probably as close as I could ever get to my homeland.

***

When I lived in Israel, admittedly, I hadn't been at all taken with Arab music. I guess that colonial settlers are rarely interested in the indigenous culture. I loved folk music and had already established myself in Europe and the USA as a klezmer player, and over the years I had begun playing Turkish and Greek music as well. Yet I had completely skipped over Arab music, and Palestinian music in particular. In London, hanging out in those Lebanese restaurants, it began to occur to me that I had never really explored the music of my neighbours. More worrisomely, I had ignored and even dismissed it. Though it had been all around me, I had never really *listened* to it. It had been there at every corner of my life: the call to prayer from the mosques, the voices of Umm Kulthum, Farid El-Atrash and Abdel Halim Hafez. It could be heard in the streets, on TV, in the small cafés in Jerusalem's Old City, in the restaurants. It had been all around me – but I had disrespectfully never given it any notice.

In my mid-thirties, away from the Middle East, I became drawn to the indigenous music of my homeland. It wasn't easy; it was, in fact, on the verge of being completely unfeasible. As much as jazz was easy for me to absorb, Arab music was almost impossible. I would put the music on, grab my saxophone or clarinet, try to integrate my sound with it and come out sounding utterly foreign. I soon realised that Arab music was a different language altogether. I didn't know where to start, or how to approach it.

To a certain extent, Jazz music is a western product with an extensive Afro-Cuban influence. It evolved at the beginning of the twentieth century and developed at the margins of American culture. Bebop, the music I grew up on, consists of relatively short fragments of music. The tunes are short because they had to fit into the three-minute record format of the 1940s. Western music can be easily transcribed into some visual content via standard notation and chord symbols. Jazz, like most Western musical forms, is therefore partially digital. Arab music, on the other hand, is analogue – it cannot be transcribed. Its authenticity evaporates in the attempt. By the time I achieved enough humane maturity to literally 'face the music' of my homeland, my musical knowledge stood in the way.

I couldn't understand what it was that stopped me from mastering Arab music, or why it didn't sound right when I tried to play it. I had spent enough time listening and practising, but it just didn't work. As time went by, European music journalists began to appreciate my new sound and to regard me as a new jazz 'hero' who crossed the divide as an expert in Arab music. I knew they were wrong though – much as I had indeed tried to cross this so-called 'divide', I could easily tell that my sound and interpretation were foreign to true Arab music.

Then I discovered an easy trick. During my concerts, when trying to emulate this elusive Oriental sound, I would first sing a line that reminded me of the sounds I had ignored in my childhood. I would try to recall the echoing call of the *muezzin* sneaking its way into our streets from the surrounding valleys, and the astonishing, haunting sounds of my friends Dhafer Youssef and Nizar Al-Issa, as well as the low, lingering voice of Abel Halim Hafez. Initially I would just close my eyes and listen with my internal ear, but without realising it, I began to gradually open my mouth as well, and to sing loudly. Then I realised that if I sang with the saxophone in my mouth, I would arrive at a sound that closely approximated the mosques' metal horns. I had tried to draw closer to the Arab sound for so long, but now I simply forgot what I was trying to achieve and began to enjoy myself.

After a while I noticed that the echoes of Jenin, al-Quds and Ramallah began to emerge naturally from the bell of my horn. I asked myself what had happened, why it suddenly sounded genuine, and concluded that I had given up on *the primacy of the eye*, and devoted my attention instead to *the primacy of the ear*. I didn't look for inspiration on the page, for the visual or the forensic, in musical notation or chord symbols. Instead, I listened to my internal voice. Struggling with Arab music reminded me why I had begun to play music in the first place. At the end of the day, I had heard Bird on the radio, I did not see him on MTV.

Through music, and particularly my very personal struggle with Arab music, I learned to *listen*. Rather than looking at history or analysing its evolution in material terms, it is listening that stands at the core of deep comprehension. Ethical behaviour comes into play when the eyes are shut and the echoes of conscience can form a tune within one's soul. To empathise is to accept the primacy of the ear[2].

Identity vs. Identifying

Chapter 1

The Right to Elaborate

In London, in what I often define as my 'self-imposed exile', I grasped that Israel and Zionism were just parts of the wider Jewish problem.

Israel is the Jewish state, at least this is what it claims to be. Israel is largely supported by world Jewry institutionally, financially and spiritually. Zionism and Israel have become the symbolic identifiers of the contemporary Jew. And yet, in spite of Israel being the Jewish State, in spite of its vast support by Jewish lobbies around the world, hardly any commentator is courageous enough to wonder what the word Jew stands for. This question, it seems, is still taboo within Western discourse.

In this book I will try to untangle the knot. I will present a harsh criticism of Jewish politics and identity. Yet, it is crucial to mention at this early stage that there will be not a single reference to Jews as ethnicity or race. In my writing, I differentiate between Jews (the people), Judaism (the religion), and Jewish-ness (the ideology). This book doesn't deal with Jews as a people or ethnicity. If anything, my studies of the issue suggest that Jews do not form any kind of racial continuum. In short, those who are searching for blood or race-related interpretation of Zionism will have to look for it in someone else's work.

In my work, I also refrain from criticising Judaism, the religion. Instead I confront different interpretations of the Judaic code. I deal with Jewish Ideology, Jewish identity politics, and the Jewish political discourse. I ask what being a Jew entails. I am searching for the metaphysical, spiritual and socio-political connotations.

I launch my journey raising a relatively simple question. Who are the Jews? Or alternatively what do people mean when they call themselves Jews?

As far as self-perception is concerned, those who call themselves Jews could be divided into three main categories:

1. Those who follow Judaism.
2. Those who regard themselves as human beings that happen to be of Jewish origin.
3. Those who put their Jewish-ness over and above all of their other traits.

The first two categories may denote a harmless and innocent group of people.

We tend to assume that religious people are generally inspired by their beliefs and are expected to abide by some sort of a higher spiritual and ethical value system. Accordingly, Judaism can be grasped as an ethical belief system[3]. Judaism was the symbolic identifier of the Jews for at least two millennia. It is pretty lucid and coherent. In spite of the fact that currently more and more crimes are committed in the name of the Torah, Judaism as a world religion can be vindicated by suggesting that Jewish nationalist *messianism* is merely an interpretation.

The second category is also pretty innocent. One cannot choose one's origin. Ethical minds would agree that people must be respected and treated equally, regardless of their origin or their racial and ethnic background.

The third category is problematic. Its definition may sound inflammatory to some. And yet, bizarrely enough, it was the formulation given on the eve of the 20th century by Chaim Weizmann, a prominent early Zionist figure and later the first Israeli President: 'There are no English, French, German or American Jews, but only Jews living in England, France, Germany or America.' In just a few words, Weizmann managed to categorically define the essence of Jewish-ness. It is basically a 'primary quality'. You may be a Jew who dwells in England, a Jew who plays the violin or even a Jew against Zionism, but above all else you are a Jew. And this is exactly the idea conveyed by the third category.

It is about viewing Jewish-ness as the key element and the fundamental characteristic of one's being. Any other quality is secondary. This is exactly the message the early Zionists were interested in promulgating. For Weizmann, Jewish-ness was a unique quality that stopped the Jew from assimilating or disappearing into the crowd. The Jew would always remain an alien.

This line of thinking was apparent in most early Zionist writings. Jabotinsky took it even further. He was adamant that assimilation was impossible due to biological conditioning. Here is what he had to say about the German Jew: 'A Jew brought up among Germans may assume German customs, German words. He may be wholly imbued with that German fluid but the nucleus of his spiritual structure will always remain Jewish, because his blood, his body, his physical racial type are Jewish.' (Vladimir Jabotinsky, 'A Letter on Autonomy', 1904).

These racist ideas predate Nazism. Jabotinsky wasn't alone, even the Jewish Marxist Ber Borochov, who refers the Jewish condition to historical and material circumstances, suggested a remedy that was particular to Jewish people, i.e. Jewish Nationalism. An ideology in which Jews would practice some proletarian activity, namely production, yet maintain their national and cultural symptoms.

Borochov sets Jews apart from the international proletarian revolution. Why does he do this? Because Jews are uniquely Jewish or at least the Zionists tend to believe they are.

The Zionist is first and foremost a Jew. He can't be just an ordinary British citizen who happens to be of a Jewish descent. He is rather a Jew who dwells in Britain. He is a Jew who speaks English, he is a Jew who receives his health services from the NHS, he is a Jew who happens to drive on the left side of the road. Though he is British by birth he is also the 'ultimate other' by choice.

Zionist Agent

This third category of Jew doesn't have to move to Palestine. Dwelling in Zion is merely one possibility offered by the Zionist philosophy. In order to become a proper Zionist you don't have to wander. Sometimes it is actually better if you stay exactly where you are.

Let us read what Victor Ostrovsky, a deserter ex-Mossad agent, is telling us about Jewish brotherhood. 'The next day Ran S. delivered a lecture on the *sayanim*, a unique and important part of the Mossad's operation. *Sayanim* (assistants) - must be 100 percent Jewish. They live abroad, and though they are not Israeli citizens, many are reached through their relatives in Israel. An Israeli with a relative in England, for example, might be asked to write a letter telling the person bearing the letter that he represents an organization whose main goal is to help save Jewish people in the Diaspora. Could the British relative help in any way? ... There are thousands of *sayanim* around the world. In London alone, there are about 2,000 who are active, and another 5,000 on the list. They fulfill many different roles. A car *sayan*, for example, running a rental agency, could help the Mossad rent a car without having to complete the usual documentation. An apartment *sayan* would find accommodation without raising suspicions, a bank *sayan* could get you money if you needed it in the middle of the night, a doctor *sayan* would treat a bullet wound without reporting it to the police, and so on. The idea is to have a pool of people available when needed who can provide services but will keep quiet about them out of loyalty to the cause. They are paid only costs.' [4]

Sayanim belong to the third category. They are people who regard themselves primarily as Jews. The *sayan* is a person who would betray the nation of which he is a citizen out of devotion to a notion of a clannish brotherhood.

While in its early days, Zionism presents itself as an attempt to bring the world Jewry to Zion, in the last three decades it has become clear to the Zionist leadership that Israel would actually benefit from world Jewry, and especially the Jewish elite, staying exactly where they are. Paul Wolfowitz[5], Rahm Emmanuel[6], Lord Levy[7] and David Aaronovitch[8] have proved far more effective for the Zionist cause by staying where they are.

Zionism, a Global Network

Zionism is not a colonial movement with an interest in Palestine, as some scholars suggest. Zionism is actually a global movement that is fuelled by a unique tribal solidarity of third category members. To be a Zionist means to accept that, more than anything else, one is primarily a Jew. Ostrovsky continues: 'You have at your disposal a non-risk recruitment system that actually gives you a pool of millions of Jewish people to tap from outside your own borders. It's much easier to operate with what is available on the spot, and *sayanim* offer incredible practical support everywhere.'[9]

What we see here is an extraordinary degree of solidarity. But Jews are far from being a single race, so if it isn't racial solidarity *per se*, what is it that leads the *sayan* to run the risk of years of imprisonment? What did Israeli spy Jonathan Pollard[10] have in mind when he betrayed his country? What do those alleged 2,000 *sayanim* in London have in mind when they betray their Queen or their neighbour? What did Paul Wolfowitz have in mind when he set the strategy for his country to demolish the last pockets of Arab resistance to Israel?

I regard Ostrovsky's testimony as a reliable report. As we know, the Israeli government used every possible means to stop the publication of his books.

In a radio interview Joseph Lapid, at the time a senior Israeli columnist, opened his heart and told the world what he thought of Ostrovsky: 'Ostrovsky is the most treacherous Jew in modern Jewish history. And he has no right to live, except if he's prepared to return to Israel and stand trial.'[11]

Valerie Pringle, the journalist on the other side of the line, asked Lapid: 'Do you feel it's a responsible statement to say what you've said?'

Lapid: 'Oh yes, I fully believe in that. And unfortunately the Mossad cannot do it because we cannot endanger our relations with Canada. But I hope there will be a decent Jew in Canada who does it for us.'

Pringle: 'You hope this. You could live with his blood on your hands?'

Lapid: 'Oh no. It's to...only it will not be his blood on my hands. It will be justice to a man who does the most horrible thing that any Jew can think of, and that is that he's selling out the Jewish state and the Jewish people for money to our enemies. There is absolutely nothing worse that a human being, if he can be called a human being, can do'.

Lapid, later a member of Sharon's cabinet, makes it very clear: to be a Jew is a deep commitment that goes far beyond any legal or moral order. Clearly, for Lapid, Jewish-ness is not a spiritual or religious stand, it is a political commitment. It is a worldview that applies to every last Jew on this planet. As he says: the Mossad can't really kill Ostrovsky, thus it is down to a 'decent Jew in Canada' to do the job.

An Israeli journalist and later an Israeli Minister of Law is here expressing the most outrageous of views. He encourages a fellow Jew to commit a murder in the name of Jewish brotherhood. In short, not only does Lapid affirm Ostrovsky's report about the world of *sayanim*, he also confirms Weizmann's view that, from a Zionist point of view, there are no Canadian Jews but only Jews who live in Canada. However, he also states that a Jew who lives in Canada would act as an assassin, serving what he regards as the Jewish cause. In Zionist eyes Jewish-ness is an international network operation.

In his book, Ostrovsky refers to it as racial solidarity; I call it third category brotherhood and Weizmann calls it Zionism. But it all means the same thing. It is all about commitment, one that pulls more and more Jews into an obscure, dangerous and unethical fellowship. Apparently, Zionism is not about Israel. Israel is just a volatile territorial asset, violently maintained by a mission force composed of Hebrew-speaking, third category Jews. In fact, there is no geographical centre to the Zionist endeavor. It is hard to determine where Zionist decisions are made. Is it in Jerusalem? In the Knesset, in the Israeli PM office, in the Mossad, or maybe in the ADL[12] offices in America? It could be in Bernie Madoff's[13] office or somewhere else in Wall Street.

The Organism

It is of course possible that there is no decision-making process at all. It is more than likely that 'Jews' do not have a centre or headquarters. It is more than likely that they aren't aware of their particular role within the entire system, the way an organ is not aware of its role within the complexity of the organism.[14] No single operator within the collective is fully familiar with the collective's operative mode but is only aware of his or her personal and limited role, function or duties within it. This is probably the Zionist movement's greatest strength. It transformed the Jewish tribal mode into a collective functioning system.

Looking at Zionism as an *organismus* would lead to a major shift in our perspective of current world affairs. The Palestinians, for instance, aren't just the victims of the Israeli occupation, they are actually the victims of a unique global political identity, namely the third category people who transformed the Holy Land into a Jewish bunker. The Iraqis are better seen as the victims of those third category infiltrators within British and

American administrations, who succeed in transforming the American and British armies into a Zionist mission force. The Muslim world should be seen as subject to the third category attempt to make 'moral interventionism' ideology into the new Western expansionist Bible. Americans and Brits and, to a certain extent, the West are all subject to a financial turmoil known as the 'credit crunch'. It could be seen as a Zio-punch.

Chapter 2

Credit Crunch or Zio Punch?

Back in 1992, the United States Secretary of Defense, Dick Cheney, appointed Paul Wolfowitz (Undersecretary for Defence Policy at the time) and his deputy Lewis 'Scooter' Libby, to draft the USA Defense Planning Guidance (DFG) for the 1994-99 fiscal years. The document that was later named as the '"Wolfowitz Doctrine"' was soon leaked to the New York Times and raised some harsh criticism.

This astonishing document laid out the strategy for merging American and global Zionist interests into a unified practice. It all happened in the wake of the collapse of the Soviet Union, as America was becoming the single super power.

'Our first objective,' wrote Wolfowitz, 'is to prevent the re-emergence of a new rival, either on the territory of the former Soviet Union or elsewhere, that poses a threat of the order of that posed formerly by the Soviet Union.'[15]

As much as Wolfowitz may claim to believe in 'freedom' and the 'free market', he states that America should not allow anyone to question its primacy in the market and the new world order.

'The U.S. must show the leadership necessary to establish and protect a new order that holds the promise of convincing potential competitors that they need not aspire to a greater role or pursue a more aggressive posture to protect their legitimate interests.'

Wolfowitz had already realised, in 1992, that the world might be reluctant to support his visionary American expansionist philosophy. America, according to him, should therefore adopt a unilateral assertive practice. Rather than counting on international coalitions and UN initiatives, America had better get used to the idea that it would have to act alone. Seemingly, already in 1992, Wolfowitz had appointed America as the World Police.

'Like the coalition that opposed Iraqi aggression, we should expect future coalitions to be ad hoc assemblies, often not lasting beyond the crisis being confronted, and in many cases carrying only general agreement over the objectives to be accomplished. Nevertheless, the sense that the world order is ultimately backed by the U.S. will be an important stabilizing factor.'

Hence, Wolfowitz stresses, America should intervene when and where it believed necessary. But then the Global Zionist pops out. Wolfowitz and Libby reaffirmed U.S. commitments to the Jewish State.

'In the Middle East and Persian Gulf, we seek to foster regional stability, deter aggression against our friends and interests in the region, protect U.S. nationals and property, and safeguard our access to international air and seaways and to the region's oil. The United States is committed to the security of Israel and to maintaining the qualitative edge that is critical to Israel's security.'

The Project for the New American Century

Wolfowitz's 'draft' soon led to the foundation of the most powerful think tank in Washington: the Project For The New American Century (PNAC), which lasted from early 1997 to 2006 and exerted a major influence within President George Bush's administration. It would be impossible to analyse American policy and the neoconservative expansionist wars during this time without taking into account the influence of the PNAC. It would also be impossible to understand the collapse of global American hegemony (in general) and in the Middle East (in particular) without bearing in mind the interventionist philosophy advocated by the PNAC and its support of Israeli global and regional interests.

According to the PNAC's homepage, the think tank's goal was 'to promote American global leadership.'[16] Following the interventionist precept set by Wolfowitz and Libby, PNAC believed that 'American leadership was both good for America and good for the world'[17]. It openly suggested that everything that was good for the Americans was also good for the rest of humanity[18].

The New American think-tankers clearly had their eyes on Iraq's oil. However Iraq also presented a constant risk to the Americans' beloved ally in the region, the Jewish state, to whom Iraq was one of the last defiant enemies. Regime change in Iraq remained the consistent position of PNAC throughout 1997-2000. Wolfowitz, who naturally emerged as a leading figure within the PNAC, put constant pressure on Clinton's adminis-tration, advocating the immediate removal of Saddam Hussein and his regime.

In 2002-2003, as America and Britain were preparing for a war against Iraq, it became evident that Bush's administration complied with PNAC's political philosophy.

As we know, the war turned into a complete disaster. For many political analysts it symbolises the beginning of the end of the American Empire. By the end of 2006, there wasn't much left of the notorious neoconservative think-tank. The PNAC was reduced to a voice-mailbox and a ghostly website, with a single employee left to wrap things up. The members of the notorious think tank quietly disappeared; some settled in far less glorious academic and administrative political posts, others just retired or faded away. Yet their philosophy left more than one and a half million fatalities in Iraq. It left one billion Muslims outraged and hostile to America's relentless expansionism. Before long the entire American geopolitical philosophy collapsed as the Arab masses identified America as their enemy, and some of the Arab tyrants as American collaborators.

Obviously knowing what we know today about Neocon

'moralist' interventional inclinations and PNAC advocacy of expansionism, such devastating consequences shouldn't take us by surprise. Yet, questions must be asked: How is it that America didn't find, within its 'free media' and political establishment, the means to resist Wolfowitz and Libby? After the election of George W. Bush in 2000, a number of PNAC's members or signatories were appointed to key positions within the President's administration. The American media and political system were very slow to react. This fact alone raises a crucial question.

How did America allow itself be enslaved by ideologies inherently associated with foreign interests?

Oil is important

The United States of America is a big country with big roads and many thirsty cars. Consequently, cheap oil is the key for its social and economical stability. Wolfowitz, Libby and PNAC, so it seemed at the time, found their way to heaven. They were about to kill two birds with just a single war. They planned to rob the Arab oil and to simultaneously 'secure' their beloved Jewish state.

As we all know, the plan didn't work out. In spite of the 2003 invasion, America didn't manage to put its heavy hand on Iraqi oil. Reconstruction of Iraq, another attempt to bank some cash, is 'yet' to happen.

However, Wolfowitz didn't fail entirely. He succeeded in destroying one fierce enemy of Israel. He toppled Saddam Hussein. But it looks as if Saddam, on his way down, managed to pull the entire American Empire and what was left of the British one, with him. Moreover, by the time the last American soldier is evacuated or air lifted from the Green Zone (Baghdad) it will be clear that it was actually the failure of Wolfowitz's doctrine that made Iran into the leading regional superpower.

The Greenspan Doctrine - Money Makes The World Go Round

How is it that America failed to restrain its Wolfowitzes? How is it that America let its foreign policy be shaped by some ruthless Zio-driven think tanks? How come alleged American 'free media' failed to warn the American people of the enemy within?

Money probably provides one answer, it does indeed make the world go round, or at least the 'American housing market'.

Throughout the centuries, some Jewish bankers have gathered the reputation of backers and financers of wars[19] and even one communist revolution[20]. Though some rich Jews have been happily financing wars using their own assets, Alan Greenspan, the Chairman of the Federal Reserve of the United States, found a far more sophisticated way to facilitate or at least divert the attention from the wars perpetrated by Libby, Wolfowitz and PNAC.

Unlike old-fashioned Britain, where Tony Blair recruited Lord Levy to encourage his 'Friends of Israel' to donate their money to a party that was just about to launch a criminal war, in America Alan Greenspan provided his president with an astonishing economic boom. It seems that the prosperous conditions at home divert the attention from the disastrous war in Iraq.

Greenspan is not an amateur economist, he knew what he was doing. He knew very well that as long as Americans were doing well, buying and selling homes, his President would be able to continue implementing the 'Wolfowitz doctrine' and PNAC philosophy, destroying the 'bad Arabs' in the name of 'democracy', 'liberalism', 'ethics', and even 'women's rights'.

Greenspan advised the American people to buy – he repeated the old mantra: 'spending is patriotic'. He also managed to convince them that if they did not have the money, that shouldn't stop them. They would 'pay later'. To a certain extent he was correct, we are all having to 'pay later'... we may even never stop paying.

Without going too deeply into economics, it was Greenspan who through some excessive deregulation prepared the monetary ground for the rise of the subprime mortgage companies: a lending market that specialises in high-risk mortgages and loans.

'Innovation,' said Greenspan in April 2005, 'has brought about a multitude of new products, such as subprime loans and niche credit programs for immigrants.'[21]

It is almost touching to find out that Greenspan cares so much about immigrants.

'Such developments,' continues Greenspan, 'are representative of the market responses that have driven the financial services industry throughout the history of our country ... With these advances in technology, lenders have taken advantage of credit-scoring models and other techniques for efficiently extending credit to a broader spectrum of consumers.'

Greenspan admits that he is leading the American banking system into an 'innovative' experiment: 'Where once the more marginal applicants would simply have been denied credit, lenders are now able to quite efficiently judge the risk posed by individual applicants and to price that risk appropriately.'

It seems the entire Western economy is paying the price for Greenspan's non-scientific notion of 'appropriately'.

'These improvements have led to rapid growth in subprime mortgage lending; indeed, today subprime mortgages account for roughly ten percent of the number of all mortgages outstanding, up from just one or two percent in the early 1990s.'

Like Wolfowitz, Greenspan had a plan. Like Wolfowitz's war it even worked for a while, but somehow it didn't work all the way through. As we all remember President Bush's embarrassing declaration of victory in Iraq, we also know that it didn't take long for the American people to acknowledge that America would never win in this war. Similarly, Greenspan had some initial numbers to be proud of. The subprime borrowing he pushed for was a major contributor to an increase in home ownership and the demand for housing. The overall U.S. homeownership rate increased from 64 percent in 1994 to a peak in 2004 with an all-time high of 69.2 percent. Real estate had become the leading business in America, more and more speculators invested money in the business. During 2006, 22 percent of homes purchased (1.65 million units) were for investment purposes, with an additional 14 percent (1.07 million units) purchased as vacation homes.

These figures led Americans to believe that their economy was indeed booming. And when an economy is booming nobody is really interested in foreign affairs, certainly not in a million dead Iraqis. But then the grave reality dawned on the many struggling, working class Americans and immigrants, who were failing to pay back money they didn't have in the first place.

Due to the rise in oil prices and the rise of interest rates, millions of disadvantaged Americans fell behind. By the time they drove back to their newly purchased suburban dream houses, there was not enough money in the kitty to pay the mortgage or elementary needs. Consequently, within a very short time, millions of houses were repossessed. Clearly, there was no one around who could afford to buy those newly repossessed houses. Consequently, the poor people of America became poorer than ever.

Just as Wolfowitz's toppled Saddam, who dragged the American Empire down with him, the poor Americans, that were set to facilitate Wolfowitz's war, pulled down American capitalism as well as the American monetary and banking system. Greenspan's policy led an entire class to ruin, leaving America's financial system with a hole that now stands at a trillion dollars.

Greenspan and Wolfowitz remind me of the joke about an insensitive surgeon who comes out of the theatre after a 12 hour heart operation, telling the anxious family 'the operation was a great success but unfortunately your beloved didn't make it to the end.'

The Moral Agenda

Greenspan and Wolfowitz's doctrines looked promising on paper. The operation was indeed successful but the American Empire didn't make it to the end. It is now doomed to lose its primacy. Greenspan, so he says, did it all for the 'immigrants' and the 'poor'. Wolfowitz appointed Great America to be the global police force. He did it for the Iraqis, for 'morality' and democracy. At least this is what he wants us to believe. The pattern is familiar, a few 'graceful' people who always try to save the world in the name of one ideal or another. They 'bring' democracy to the 'savage', they 'bring' equality to the poor. They employ abstract ethical concepts. But somehow, the Jewish state is always set to benefit. One just has to read the first and prominent Zionist prophet Theodor Herzl to know that this is what political Zionism is all about: getting superpowers to serve the Zionist cause.

Some Americans were fooled into blindly following Wolfowitz and Greenspan, many others, especially in the highest economical, political and media echelons, were stupid not to stop them in time. Greenspan and Wolfowitz should have at least been restrained. Already in 1992 Americans should have been alerted to the possible dangers concerning foreign interests within the hub of their strategic headquarters.

You may wonder at this stage whether I regard the credit crunch as a Zionist plot or even a Jewish conspiracy. In fact the opposite is the case. It isn't a plot and certainly not a conspiracy for it was all in the open. It is actually an accident. The patient didn't make it to the end.

Chapter 3

Zionism and Other Marginal Thoughts

One way to look into marginal politics is to illuminate the problematic tension between demands for equality and the maintenance of clannish or tribal worldviews. I am referring here to the difficult duality involved in wanting to be seen as everyone else while considering oneself to be different, unique or even superior. At first glance, it seems as if a humanist and universal demand to equalise civil rights would address the issue and resolve any form of tension between the margin and the centre. But marginal politics intends to defy any call for equalisation. For the marginal politician, assimilation, emancipation, integration and even liberation are death threats.

Once assimilated[22] or integrated[23], the margin faces a severe 'identity crisis'. The marginal subject is asked to renounce his or her particularity, uniqueness and singularity. Following integration or assimilation, the heroic 'pre-revolutionary' days of the righteous struggle for equality or civil rights are replaced by a nostalgic narrative. In its post-revolutionary phase, what had once been the margin becomes an unnoticeable entity, an ordinary crowd. Thus, we should deduce that the demand for equality is in itself a self-defeating mechanism. Once equal, one is no different from anyone else. The success of integration reduces the marginal discourse to a meaningless noise. No marginal politician endorses a political call for assimilation. Such a call would mean political suicide, a self-imposed destruction of one's political power.

By contrast, we can easily conceive of individuals wanting to assimilate; we can envisage a member of the so-called margin searching for ways to integrate within mainstream society. A glimpse into the social reality of pre-Second World War European Jews provides an interesting insight into the issue. For the reasons stated above, assimilation has never been presented as a Jewish political call. It was rather individual Jews who welcomed and enjoyed European liberal tendencies. The Jewish political call was inspired by different means of tribal, cultural or even racially-orientated segregation. A survey of our surrounding Western reality reveals an image of multiplicity. Our society is an amalgam in which many who were once marginal are now assimilated and integrated. Moreover, various minorities do not even regard their integration as a conscious process but rather as a celebration of being amongst others. This natural tendency to merge with one's surrounding society is seen by the marginal politician as a major threat.

The Margin

'The margin' is a term that often refers to those who, somehow, live on the edge of society. It describes those who fall behind, those who cannot express their voice within mainstream discourse. The margin is often oppressed, harassed, humiliated, subject to despicable jokes, stereotypes and so forth. The margin retains its marginal qualities as long as the injustices committed against it are not addressed within the mainstream discourse. Once the particularity and the uniqueness of the margin is recognised and accepted by the crowd, the margin becomes an inherent part of the larger community, in other words, it becomes a minority group or even an integral, indistinguishable part of the mainstream.

Hence, it should be accepted that the state of being marginal is, at least to a certain extent, defined by the centre. But can the margin also be defined politically on its own terms? Is being a lesbian, for instance, enough for one to be 'marginal' regardless of the surrounding social circumstances? How does one decide whether one belongs to any given margin? Is being a Jew, a

Muslim, gay or an ethnic Albanian enough to make one a 'marginal identity'?

Clearly not. We can think of many Jews, Muslims, gays, lesbians and ethnic Albanians who detach themselves from any form of marginal or identity politics. They do not see themselves as marginal, nor are they seen as such by their surrounding environment. Moreover, some of the so-called marginal groups are, by far, over represented in politics and media. Jews for instance cannot really complain about their political voice being silenced or unheard. The margin, therefore, is a dynamic notion and it is shaped by its relationship with the centre. The margin is defined in terms of negation (i.e. what it isn't) rather than by its positive qualities (i.e. what it is). This is why marginal politics depicts reality in terms of binary oppositions.

For the gay ideologist the binary opposition is gay/heterosexual; for the feminist politician it is femininity/masculinity; for the Zionist it is Jew/gentile and *Eretz Yisrael*/Diaspora.

As soon as the centre is willing to expand its perception of itself, introducing more liberal and inclusive thoughts, the margin's discourse confronts a threat of extinction. This is the point at which marginal and identity politics interferes and the binary opposition is introduced. The marginal politician is engaged in the maintenance of negation. This negation usually comes into play by the evocation of a conflict between the margin and the centre.

Zionism, for instance, is maintained by anti-Semitism. This may explain why Zionists are so enthusiastic about the growing statistics of anti-Semitic incidents. Similarly, gay marginal politics is fueled by homophobia and feminism thrives on the male chauvinist. Marginal and identity politics are destined to engage in an exchange with mainstream discourse. But it can never reconcile. It is there to retain negation. And yet, the question remains: can the marginal define itself by its own means? In order to address this question we must first grasp the notion of identity.

Identity, Identification and Authenticity

In order to transform the 'marginal' into a meaningful notion, the marginal subject must assume that being a 'marginal subject' conveys a significant, real and authentic identity. An American Jewish settler living on confiscated Palestinian land must genuinely believe that being on occupied land, being involved in war crimes and breaching every possible moral code on a daily basis, while risking his own life and the lives of members of his family, constitutes the direct fulfillment of his 'true self'. The settler must believe that he is the son of Abraham, and that this relation to his ancestor grants him special rights where Palestinian land is concerned.

Belief in an authentic identity is crucial for the realisation of the self as a genuine autonomous agent, but is authenticity possible? A phenomenological thinker may say yes. Edmund Husserl argues that we can refer to 'Evidez', which is 'awareness' of matter itself, as disclosed in the most clear, distinct and adequate way for something of its kind. Accordingly, one can experience a pure awareness of oneself. This notion was articulated by Descartes' 'cogito ergo sum': 'I think therefore I am.' In phenomenological terms, it is the pure and lucid 'awareness' of 'me thinking' which removes any doubt concerning me 'being in the world', at least as a thinking entity.

Phenomenology attempts to describe how the world is constituted and experienced through conscious acts, and what is given to us in immediate experience without being mediated by preconceptions and theoretical notions. From a phenomenological perspective, one's self-awareness can depict an unmediated, authentic form of knowledge.

It didn't take long for Husserl's student Martin Heidegger to expose major cracks in his teacher's philosophical endeavour. Heidegger revealed that 'being in the world' might be slightly more complex than Husserl had suggested. It was the former's notion of hermeneutics that exposed the shortcomings of Husserl's phenomenology. Hermeneutics deals with the subtle interaction between the interpreting subject and the interpreted object. Within his critical reading of Husserl, Heidegger exposed the embarrassing fact that unmediated awareness is actually hard to conceive. Human beings, it appears, do 'belong to language'. Language is out there before one comes to the world. Once one enters the realm of language, a separating wall made of symbolic linguistic bricks and cultural mortar blocks one's access to any possible 'unmediated awareness'. Can we think without applying language? Can we experience at all without the mediation of language?

Admittedly, we are capable of feeling desire while dreaming or being overwhelmed by beauty, but then, as soon as we think it through, we find ourselves entangled in a process of naming. As soon as we name, the alleged 'unmediated' is lost forever. Once within the realm of language, our perception of the world is shaped by meanings and symbols that are not uniquely ours. It would seem that a comprehensive authentic awareness is unattainable. If this is indeed the case, there is no longer room to talk about identity in terms of a genuine expression of a 'real-self'. As soon as we name, we surrender to language. Hence, looking into oneself can never reveal an authentic identity.

Alternatively, we may be able to think of identity as a set of ideas, narratives, 'thinking modes' or behavioural code. But then rather than really talking in terms of a genuine 'self-awareness', we are proceeding into a new territory. Consequently we identify with ideas, narratives, thinking modes, certain worldviews, perceptions, physical identifiers and so on. But then we must also accept that 'identity' refers to 'identification'. Instead of any form of true authentic 'self seeking,' we are engaged in some sort of affiliation. The notion of identity, which is so crucial for post-modernists, identity politics and marginal theoreticians, is nothing but a myth or a fantasy. When we refer to 'marginal identity', what we really mean is a form of identification. Thus, being homosexual is not enough to turn one into a 'gay'. While being homosexual refers to sexual preference being a 'gay' is a form of (marginal) identification i.e. a powerful affinity to a group rather than to the self.

Seemingly, the marginal subject cannot define itself by its own means. It is defined by negation. It is defined by an existing symbolic order. Rather than finding a 'real self', it is an exchange with the world, which brings identity politics to life. When talking about identity we refer to an axis of identification: at one pole we find the elusive notion of authenticity produced by a myth of unmediated self-awareness, at the other pole we find a state of estrangement that is achieved by identification (a conceptual or symbolic affinity). Thus, the search for one's genuine identity should be associated with utter misery: the more one searches for one's authentic self the more one is engaged in the process of identification that will eventually lead to complete alienation. Here I turn to Lacan's subversive twist on Descartes' *cogito*, in which 'I think therefore I am' becomes 'You are where you do not think.' If anything, thinking removes one from oneself.

Identity Politics and Marginal Philosophies

The statement: 'I look into myself and see a Zionist, a gay, a woman, a nation, a watermelon,' and so on, really means: I identify with Zionism, gays, women, certain politics and so on. Once we think, we are already defeated by the dictatorial power of language. Marginal communities and identity political discourses are generally very sensitive to the power of language, and this is probably the reason why a substantial amount of marginal political effort is dedicated to imposing lingual restrictions within the mainstream discourse (usually in the name of political correctness, liberalism and even tolerance).

This is also likely to be why marginal communities are so creative in their use of language. The Zionists' relationship with the resurrected Hebrew language is a good example. Early Zionists realised that full control over language would allow them to impose their worldview on subsequent generations of Jews. But Zionists are not alone in this respect. Other marginal groups are known for their creative dialects, spelling and vocabulary. The following list presents different spellings for the word woman/women used by lesbian separatists in the 1970s: wimmin, wimyn, womyn, womin. These alternative spellings were intended to 'prove' that, at least symbolically, woman could be 'complete' even when the word man/men was taken out of woman/women. 'We, as womyn, are not a sub-category of men.'[24] The meaning defines the worldview. But then, if language has such a crucial role in marginal politics, the margin can never detach itself from the centre. Even when it establishes its own discourse, lingual signs and symbolic order, this discourse can only be realised in terms of its relationship and exchange with mainstream discourse.

The Strategies

Since the possibility of assimilation is occasionally presented to the margin by the hegemony, opportunities for integration within the centre are occasionally available to the marginal subject. Assimilated Jewish Americans, for instance, have always been extremely excited about the possibility of becoming American patriots. Many American Jews have found their way into the leading classes via the academic world, banking, real estate, the stock market, the media, politics and so on. But once they are in key positions within mainstream society, their patriotic tendencies are challenged by those they left in the margins.

Zionist lobbies in America specialise in tracing rich and influential Jews. They pressurise them to 'come out of the closet' and to show greater commitment to the Jewish nationalist venture. Interestingly enough, gay marginal politicians behave similarly. Some marginal politicians seek to publicly 'shame' their integrated brothers and sisters.

This serves two purposes. First, it conveys a clear message that real assimilation is impossible: once a gay, always a gay; once a Jew always a Jew. This logic was reflected in a Hollywood cinematic cartoon, Shrek. Shrek and Princess Fiona were doomed to find out that 'Once an ogre always an ogre. One can never escape one's real identity.' And yet Shrek and Princess Fiona are loved by their friends for being humane in spite of their being ogres.

Second, it pushes the assimilated being towards collaboration with his old clan. You will never escape who you are so you better be proud of it. The American Zionist takes this ideology one step further, telling the assimilated Jew: 'You will never escape who you are so why not be proud of it and work for us.' These points help us understand the impact of Jewish and Israeli lobbies within Western politics.[25] Earlier on we read the words of Israeli Journalist Joseph Lapid, calling Diaspora Jews to assassinate Mossad deserter Ostrovsky for telling the truth about Israel. The marginal agitator seems to demand compliance.

Let us review the logic behind this strategy. Chaim Weizmann's statement regarding English, French and German Jews being primarily Jews is obviously a call for Jews to celebrate their sameness. Being Jewish, according to Weizmann, is an essential characteristic; all other qualities are almost contingent. Thus it would seem that even the 'good Jews', those who protest against Israeli atrocities while shouting 'not in my name', fall into Weizmann's trap. First they are Jews and only then are they humanists. In practice, without realising it, they adopt Weizmann's marginal anti-assimilationist strategy. Weizmann's strategy is sophisticated and hard to tackle. Even saying 'I do not agree with Israel although I am a Jew' is to fall into the trap.

Having fallen into the trap, one cannot leave the clan behind – one can hardly endorse a universal philosophy while being identified politically as a Jew.

In the early days of Zionism, most Jews refused to buy Weizmann's agenda – they preferred to see themselves as American, British or French people who happened to be Jewish. This dispute between the Western Diaspora ethnic Jew and the Zionist movement developed into a bitter conflict. During their struggle for recognition, Zionists admitted their contempt for the Diaspora Jew. This was essentially the birth of Zionist separatism.

Separatism

'Before the emancipation, the Jew was a stranger among the peoples, but he did not for a moment think of making a stand against his fate. He felt himself as belonging to a race of his own, which had nothing in common with the other people of the country. The emancipated Jew is insecure in his relations with his fellow-beings, timid with strangers, suspicious even toward the secret feeling of his friends.' *Max Nordau*[26], *address at the first Zionist Congress, Basle, 1897*

The term 'separatism' refers to the process in which a minority group chooses to break away from a larger group. Separation is called for as soon as the marginal political group senses an imminent danger of integration into mainstream society. Separatism refers not only to attempts to create alternative societies, but also to exclusionary practices within marginal communities themselves.

Zionism developed as a reaction to the emancipation of European Jewry, a process that started with the French Revolution and spread rapidly all over Europe during the nineteenth century. By the late nineteenth century, a few prominent, assimilated Jews (such as Nordau, Herzl and

Weizmann) realised that emancipation of the Jewish people might lead to the disappearance of the Jewish identity. The Zionist argument, at the time, was simple; ghetto walls had been demolished and yet Jews were failing to integrate into European life. Additionally, the Europeans were accused of being insincerely sympathetic towards Jews. Nordau said 'The nations which emancipated the Jews have mistaken their own feelings. In order to produce its full effect, emancipation should first have been completed in sentiment before it was declared by law.'[27] The argument is of a very basic character: first you should love me and only then should you marry me. This idea appears reasonable, but we have to remember that, unlike in a love affair, civil life is based on respect rather than affection. I expect my neighbour to respect me; he may love me too but I can never demand it.

In order to support their views, Zionists created an image of emerging anti-Semitism. Their illustration was far from accurate. In fact, by the late nineteenth century, Jews were already deeply involved in every possible aspect of European civil life. Moreover, the Zionist leaders themselves were highly integrated within their Christian context. But a myth of persistent persecution was needed.

On 15 October 1894 Captain Alfred Dreyfus, the sole Jewish member of the French army's General Staff, was detained on charges of spying for Germany. Throughout his trial Dreyfus declared his innocence. For many it was clear that Dreyfus was a victim of a despicable racist allegation. Theodor Herzl, a prominent Viennese journalist who traveled to Paris to cover the trial, was moved by the saga and deduced from it that assimilation was doomed to fail. The only solution, according to Herzl, was '[a] promised land, where we can have hooked noses, black or red beards ... without being despised for it, where we can live at least as free men on our own soil, and where we can die peacefully in our own fatherland' (Judenstaat, Theodor Herzl). In fact the Dreyfus trial created a huge surge of gentile support. The French government eventually bowed to public pressure and reduced his sentence. Following the support of French intellectuals and the European left, Zionism lost its grip in France. The French Jews felt truly emancipated. Herzl's displeasure was evident in the following extract from his diary: '[French Jews] seek protection from the socialists and the destroyers of the present civil order ... truly they are not Jews anymore. To be sure, they are not Frenchmen either. They will probably become the leaders of European anarchism.'

It would appear that Herzl, a marginal politician, sensed better than anyone else the imminent threat of Jewish integration and assimilation. This example illustrates the essence of separatist ideologies – the aim to put barriers between people. Separatism is a strategy of ghetto-building and Zionists have followed this strategy since the late nineteenth century.

The case of lesbian separatism is very similar. In the 1970s, when women were closing social gaps and achieving greater equality, a radical militant feminism emerged. In her article 'The Way of All Separatists'[28], Ludo McFingers writes: 'They hate men, see women as a sex class, support biological determinism, reject reformism and despise the left.'

The underlying premise of lesbian separatism is that men cannot or will not change. Consequently, women can only guarantee their own freedom by detaching themselves from men. Some separatist women even suggest a need for violent confrontation with men to overthrow their power. Not surprisingly some of the most radical lesbian separatists would prefer to live in a world entirely free of men and some have gone so far as to state that 'Dead men don't rape'. This echoes the Israeli popular expression: 'A good Arab is a dead Arab.'

The similarities between Zionist and feminist separatists are evident. Moreover, from time to time the two radical ideologies merge into a single voice. When it was suggested to the

American Jewish feminist Andrea Dworkin that the idea of *Womenland* was insane she answered: 'Didn't they say that about Israel? And didn't the world think that Theodor Herzl, the founder of the Zionist movement, was a crank? The Jews got a country because they had been persecuted, said that enough was enough, decided what they wanted and went out and fought for it. Women should do the same. And if you don't want to live in Womenland, so what? Not all Jews live in Israel, but it is there, a place of potential refuge if persecution comes to call ... as the Jews fought for Israel so women have the right to execute – that's right, execute – rapists and the state should not intervene.'[29] Earlier in the same interview, Dworkin, whom the Guardian defined as a 'far left' activist, admitted that she 'remains a supporter of Israel's right to exist, of the Jewish right to have their own state and the Jewish right to fight back against those who tried and still try to kill them; just as she thinks that women have the right to fight back, even kill, the men who have abused them.' Dworkin may represent the views of a tiny and insignificant minority but the ideological similarities between Zionism and Feminist Separatism are clear. One significant difference, however, is that Israel possesses hundreds of nuclear bombs.

A long time ago I found that through the replacement of the word 'woman' with 'Jew' and the word 'man' with 'gentile', a lesbian separatist text could be transformed smoothly into a radical Zionist pamphlet and vice versa. Lesbian separatism is a form of 'ultimate feminism'; it requires a shift from the realisation that 'every woman can be a lesbian' to the radical perception that 'every woman should be a lesbian.'[30] Similarly, a Zionist would argue that 'every Jew should be a Zionist' rather than that 'every Jew can be a Zionist'. Some Zionists would go further and argue that since Israel is 'the state of the Jewish people' every Jew should be seen as a Zionist. Accordingly, rejection of Zionism by a Jew should be considered an act of treason, or at very least a form of self-hatred.

Naturally, most women would not seriously accept their categorisation by radical feminists. I would say that, at least before the Second World War, the majority of Jews were offended by the Zionist call. It appears that the Holocaust, its exploitation and the unprecedented 1967 Israeli military victory changed the attitude of world Jewry towards Zionism and Israel.

The Holocaust was a 'Zionist victory', just as each single rape is interpreted by feminist separatist ideologists as a verification of their theories. As we have seen, marginal politics is maintained by hostility against oneself. In order to sustain marginal politics, the loathing directed against oneself becomes advantageous. Zionists rely upon burned synagogues and some lesbian separatists agitators rely upon rape victims. If there were no burned synagogues around, Mossad would go as far as burning some itself[31]. Within the separatist worldview, such behaviour is legitimate because the end is far more important than the means, and the campaign is more important than any moral integrity.

Chapter 4

The *Sabra*, the Settler and the Diaspora Jew

'The Sabra, Tough and Tender – the native-born Israeli has been given a sobriquet 'Sabra' after the wild cactus which flourishes in the arid soil of Israel; the fruit of this plant is prickly on the outside and soft in the inside. This implies that our sabras are tough, brusque, inaccessible and yet surprisingly gentle and sweet within. The nickname is given affectionately and is borne with pride by our young, who enjoy the reputation that they cannot be 'savoured' from outward appearances. 'But you don't look Jewish' is the dubious compliment a young Israeli usually receives when he goes abroad. The Sabra is usually a head taller than his father, often blond and freckled, often blue eyed and snub nosed. He is cocky, robustly built, and likes to walk in open sandals in a free-swinging, lazy slouch.' *Tough and Tender, an art installation by Gabi Gofbarg, 1992*

As I pointed out in the previous chapter, marginal identities are quick to adopt behavioural codes and symbolic identifiers that make the marginal subject unmistakably distinguishable. On the surface it makes sense; the marginal subject celebrates its detachment from mainstream society or collective. It would seem as though the marginal subject was revealing its 'true self'. Yet, as discussed earlier on, the notion of a 'true manifested political identity' cannot be taken seriously. Nonetheless, we can allow ourselves to move one step forward. If the notion of the 'real self' is left out, then an external means of identification is required. Such a procedure helps the marginal subject to identify itself, but it also promotes the emerging political identity within the larger social structure.

All things considered, appearance and other symbolic identifiers, such as a special skullcap or badges, are probably far more
important than ideological depth. Marginal identities make
themselves easily distinguishable in the crowd. This applies to
the *Sabra*, the anti-Zionist Jew, the Settler, the orthodox Jew, but
also to any other marginal identity.

From a pre-1967 Zionist perspective the *Sabra* (as described
above by Gabi Gofbarg) is a separatist Jew. Not only he is
different, he also celebrates each of his differences. He is defined
in terms of negation in relation to the 'inauthentic' Diaspora Jew.
'Like a wild cactus' the *Sabra* 'flourishes in arid soil', while the
Diaspora Jew withers in Europe or America. The *Sabra* 'is prickly
on the outside and soft in the inside', while the 'speculative
capitalist' Diaspora character appears soft on the outside but is
extremely shrewd where business is concerned. The *Sabra* is
'tough and tender', he can kill like a real 'man' when he 'has to'
but this doesn't stop him from weeping at the 'Wailing Wall' as
soon as he has completed an invasion of the Old City of
Jerusalem (1967)[32]. He can ethnically cleanse the entire
Palestinian nation on Friday and then attend a 'Peace Now'
demonstration in Tel Aviv on Saturday evening. Unlike the 'soft'
Diaspora Jew, the *Sabra* is tough – he is 'a head taller than his
father'. Like a German soldier he is 'often blond ... often blue
eyed ... He is cocky, robustly built.' But then unlike a German
soldier he is loose, he likes to walk in Biblical sandals in a 'free-
swinging, lazy slouch ...'. Basically, he is a kind of a bizarre
mixture of an SS commander and a biblical Moses.

As interesting as this caricature may be, there is nothing
authentic about this construction. As an Israeli male secular Jew
between 1948 and the 1980s, one was destined to participate
'willingly' in a collective mimicking of an imaginary *Nuevo
Israelite* icon. I guess that this process alone robbed the first
Israelis of the capacity to experience anything that may resemble

authenticity. Instead they celebrated their victories through identification with a newly-born Jewish archetype.

The birth of the West Bank Settler Jew (following the 1967 war), a radical messianic militant who plans to confiscate the entire 'land of biblical Israel' in the name of God, is an attempt to bring the *Sabra* back home to the *shtetl*. It is an effort to resolve the schizophrenic *Sabra* identity. Like the *Sabra*, the settler walks in Biblical sandals in the winter; like the *Sabra* he is athletic and robustly built (until the age of twenty-two, when he grows a gigantic belly that stands as a symbol for good Jewish health). But then, unlike the *Sabra*, he has a skullcap on his head, his *Tzitzit*[33] falls out of his trousers and patches of hair cover his young face. He is far from being handsome. Needless to say, he doesn't resemble a *Wehrmacht* soldier. He looks very much like a Diaspora Jew strapped to an Uzi or M16. He looks like a Jew because he is one and he is proud to be one.

As much as the formulation of the *Sabra* identity was a secular Zionist separatist attempt within the context of emerging Jewish nationalism and Jewish identity politics, the West Bank Settler manages to establish a consistent continuum between the Jew, Judaism and Jewish-ness. The settler is a homogenous authentic being. The Settler is fuelled by coherent meanings. Even when he confiscates land or murders a Palestinian family he knows exactly what for. The Wailing Wall, for him, is a sacred place to worship his God. The settler doesn't shoot and sob; he is driven by conviction. Like the *Sabra* the settler is distinguished by a set of symbolic identifiers: knitted skullcap, Biblical sandals, *tzitzit*, an automatic rifle and a beard. Yet, each of these symbolic identifiers is intrinsically associated with his Judaic belief and the Jewish ideology he upholds. In other words, the settler has managed to bond the 'inside' i.e. the Jewish soul and the 'outside' namely the appearance, into a meaningful Jewish experience. This fact alone may explain why, along the years, the *Sabra* identity faded away, yet, the settler one matured into an Israeli political power that is extensively supported by Jewish lobbies around the world.

In historical terms, the West Bank Settler appeared on the scene just after the 1967 Israeli military victory. To a certain extent, the Settler signifies the shift of Zionism into a post-revolutionary movement; while the *Sabra* was destined to move the Jewish State from the 'dream' into a material reality, the Settler was there to fill the new reality with clear meaning. The Settler was there to bridge the gap between the Diaspora and *Eretz Yisrael*. If Zionism was initially defined as 'the negation of the Diaspora'[34], the settler was there to introduce the new Zionist phase. The settler merged all different aspects of Jewishness into a unified, organic meaning and a simple political practice. He has become the new and most popular interpretation of 'Jewish home-coming'. From a Jewish perspective, the settler has managed to move Zionism beyond its Separatist phase. It transformed Zionism into an inclusive 'Jews only' ideology. It somehow offered an ideology that united the tribe on many levels. This fact may explain the constant rise of the Right in Israel since 1967.

But here is an interesting twist. By bonding *Eretz Yisrael* and the Diaspora into a new Jewish continuum, the Settler replaces the 'negation of the Diaspora' (that was inherent to the earlier Zionist discourse) with a 'negation of the Goyim' (a return of the Jewish pre-Zionist condition). In the form of Rightwing Zionism, this ideology has matured into the most influential political force in Israel. The reason is simple – it manages to knot together Jewish politics, Judaism and Jewish tribal spirit.

Slowly but surely, this Rightwing ideology, which has its ideological roots within the Settler movement, has managed to unite most of world Jewry behind Zionism. However, this process, also regarded as the Zionification of world Jewry, is not entirely free of faults. It sets Diaspora Jews apart from their surrounding social reality. It halts the process of Jewish assimilation and instead the Jew again becomes a member of a distinct tribe with political and global interests. It also transforms the Diaspora Jewish discourse into a marginal and separatist discourse in the West. By the time a Diaspora Jew is Zionised, he or she is subject to Zionist marginal politics within their respective societies. To a certain extent, this may be seen by some as a great Zionist achievement. Yet it is far from an adequate solution to the Jewish question. It leaves the Diaspora Jew in limbo. He or she is neither assimilated into their surrounding social environment nor settled in a Jewish state.

Also, considering the racist, expansionist Judeo-centric nature of the Jewish State, the Diaspora Jew finds himself or herself intrinsically associated with a bigoted, ethnocentric ideology and an endless list of crimes against humanity.

As we can see, the Jewish political discourse is always set as a form of negation. The political Jew is always against something, or set apart from something else. This is far from being an ideal recipe for a peaceful, ethical life, driven by reconciliation and harmony.

Chapter 5

Fagin vs. Einstein

Jews are often proud to define themselves as Jews. Some Jews may, for instance, proudly carry the Jewish banner (Jews for Peace, Jews for Justice, Jews for Jesus and so on) as if they believe that the 'J' word contains special righteous attributions. However, they will also be gravely offended if they are called a 'Jew' by others. Suggesting to a Jew that 'he is a Jew' or 'behaves like a Jew' can be regarded as a serious 'racist' offence.

It is linguistically noteworthy that the symbolic identifier 'Jew' or 'Jewish' operates as both noun and as an adjective. As much as the term points to a 'thing' it is also descriptive. Symbolic identifiers associated with ideological and identity politics tend to function in dual grammatical mode. The words 'feminist', 'socialist', 'Nazi' and 'white supremacist' can point to a human subject but they can also be descriptive. For instance, a feminist who proudly carries the feminist flag may also accept that being called 'a feminist' also assigns particular character-istics and ideological beliefs. Crucially, we also accept that being a feminist, a socialist or a Nazi are matters of political choice. People are not born feminists or socialists. They adopt those ideologies or identities later in life.

From this perspective the 'Jew' signifier or symbolic identifier is slightly different for the Jews, who are born into a collective identity. Almost like any case of biologically-deter-mined conditions, such as 'women', 'men' or 'blacks', some people are born Jews. However, here there is an interesting twist. First, European Jews can easily disappear into a white Western crowd by means of assimilation and integration and leave their Jewish identity behind, whereas black people and women have to live their life accepting and enjoying who they are. Second, the duality between the noun and the adjective in the case of 'black' and 'women' is not necessarily realised as a gulf. Neither black people nor women are offended by being called 'black' or 'women'.

As discussed before, it is rather enlightening to find out that, to a certain extent, the manner in which 'Jew' as a signifier operates within the discourse may be similar to the case of the 'gay' symbolic identifier. While many gay people are proud to exhibit their gay identity, they may also be offended when being labeled as 'gays' by others. In different cases of identity and marginal politics we can notice a parallel and simultaneous tendency to 'own' and 'disown', an inclination to 'identify' with a collective yet a refusal to be 'identified' as such by others.

In multicultural reality we tend to believe that this contradictory mode of behavior is something to do with the usage and misusage of stereotypes.

A stereotype is commonly defined as a public or common belief about specific social groups, or types of individuals. It is often the product of an essentialist generalisation by the means of induction: it involves a nonscientific assumption about the properties of a class of subjects based on an accumulation of observations or anecdotal encounters, which become reinforced with time and repetition.

The concept of 'stereotype' is often confused with the notion of 'prejudice'. We notice that a stereotype attached to ethnicity, class or any group is a means of forming an opinion, usually an unfavorable one, based on insufficient knowledge and irrational feelings.

On the face of it, it would seem as if Jews are over-sensitive to the 'racial' discriminatory implication of the 'J' word. However most Jews are not that concerned when being associated collectively with some great minds, adorable violin players or conductors. In short, to safely apply the 'Jew' category, you just have to make sure you say the right things. No one will ever cause you any trouble for mentioning Albert Einstein in reference to Jewish intelligence or even bringing up Anne Frank as an exemplary motif of Jewish innocence but you may get into some serious trouble once you mention the following list of real and fictional characters: Bernie Madoff, Fagin, Wolfowitz, Lord Levy, Shylock, Alan Greenspan, Netanyahu and Nathan Rothschild.

All of the above depicts an obscure, yet far from surprising picture. It looks as if many Jews do not mind racial generalisations and essentialist stigmas as long as they are positive.

It occurred to me recently that by juxtaposing Jewish stereotypes (those which Jews seem to hate versus those which Jewish ethnic campaigners try to promote) we may be able to throw some crucial light over issues to do with Jewish collective identity. It would also suggest to us how Jews might see themselves and, even more importantly, it may also help us to grasp how they prefer to be seen.

Some Jews are rather unhappy with Charles Dickens' Fagin and Shakespeare's Shylock, who they regard as 'anti Semitic'. I get the impression that the prominent Zionist enthusiast and London solicitor Anthony Julius would like to see these cultural iconic characters removed from popular discourse. On the other hand, the British Holocaust Education Trust (HET) has managed to plant Anne Frank within the British curriculum.

It doesn't take a genius to gather why Julius and others are concerned with Fagin or Shylock. Fagin is the ultimate plunderer, a child exploiter and usurer. Shylock is the bloodthirsty merchant. With Fagin and Shylock in mind, the Israeli treatment of the Palestinians seems to be just a further event in an endless hellish continuum. However, it is also obvious why the HET is so thrilled by Anne Frank. On the face of it, and for obvious reasons, Frank is there to convey an image of innocence. And indeed not a single moral system could ever justify the ordeal this young girl went through along with many others.

Yet, Anne Frank wasn't exactly a literary genius. Her diary is not a valuable piece of literature. She wasn't exceptionally clever either. She was in fact a very ordinary girl and this is exactly her power within the post WWII Western cultural discourse. She was just an innocent, average girl. In fact, the attempt to make Anne Frank into a cultural hero may be a genuine reflection of the Jewish ideological inclination towards sameness. Frank mirrors the desperate attempt to prove to the world that 'we, the Jews' are people like other people. Moreover, the success of Anne Frank's Diary is there to suggest the West's willingness to accept Jews as people amongst peoples.

Yet, once again, the Jewish discourse is caught in a limbo. Jewish people can never achieve their task. They can never be like 'other people', for those who demand to be seen as equal must feel inherently and categorically different. Once again we face a repetition of the Jewish identity's collective unresolved chasm between 'who one claims to be' and 'what one happens to be.'

In Trials of The Diaspora, Anthony Julius attacks those whom he labels as 'anti-Semites' for being anti-Zionists. The problem with anti-Zionism, says Julius, is that 'it denies the Jews the right that it upholds for other comparable people, it adheres to the right of self-determination except in the Jews' case.... It affirms international law. Except in Israel's case. It regards Jewish nationalism (i.e. Zionism) as uniquely pernicious, rather than merely another nationalism.'[35] The cry for legitimacy and sameness in Julius' text is pretty embarrassing, especially due to the fact that the Jewish 'right of self-determination' is celebrated at the expense of someone else (the Palestinians). Zionism *is* uniquely pernicious, at least for being devastating to the indigenous population of the Holy Land.

For Julius to win his argument, Jews have to prove that they are truly the same rather than demand to be seen as similar. For Jews to be genuinely respected as a collective, self-reflection is of the essence. Instead of pointing out what is so wrong with the *Goyim*, Jewish ideologists may want to consider looking in the mirror.

Chapter 6

Think Tribal, Speak Universal

At a certain stage, around 2005, I thought to myself that I might be King of The Jews. I have achieved the unachievable, accomplished the impossible. I have managed to unite them all: Right, Left and Centre. The entirety of the primarily-Jewish British political groups: the Zionists, the anti-Zionists, Jewish Socialists, Tribal Marxists, The Board of Deputies, Jewish Trotskyites, Jews for this and Jews for that, for the first time in history all spoke in one single voice. They all hated Gilad Atzmon equally.

"Pretty impressive," I thought to myself, "I must have done something right." Yet, I was slightly confused by my own achievement. When it comes down to it, I was not the canonical enemy – I was a jazz musician and author. I was not a politician, nor was I a member of any party. I did not present or support any political agenda or power. I wasn't supported by any party either. I have never been involved in any act of violence (not even as an Israeli soldier) nor had I ever called for violence. I was what some call an 'independent critical thinker', I may also be what some Jews regard as a 'proud, self-hating Jew'. Could it be that it was my comprehension of the Jewish political identity that brought so much Jewish animosity to my door?

At the time I came across an interesting insight into the subject of anti-Semitism. It goes like this: 'While in the past an "anti-Semite" was someone who hates Jews, nowadays it is the other way around, an anti-Semite is someone the Jews hate.' The politics of hate can be effective, as well as being vicious. And you'd think tribal Jewish activists would be the first to understand this. We all know that Jews have been suffering hatred and discrimination for centuries. Yet the Jewish ethnic activists seem to have learned hatred from their enemies so well that the secular Jewish political discourse has been totally shaped by it.

Moreover, hate has become the main matrix of negation: the Israelis hate the Arabs, the Zionists hate the Goyim (in general), Jews against Zionism also hate the Goyim but they also hate Israel as well as Atzmon (in particular). But why do they hate so much? The answer is simple. Once Judaism is renounced, what remains of Jewish identity is pretty threadbare. Once stripped of religious spirituality, all that is left of Jewish-ness is a template of negation fuelled by racial orientation and spiced up with some light cultural references such as *matza* balls and chicken soup.

Sadly, I have to say that though very many emancipated and assimilated Jews have adopted universal humanist ideas and intermingled with humanity, secular collective Jewish identity has never matured into adopting a universal humanist ideological standpoint or even a philosophical insight.

The reasons are simple:

A. Racial, tribal or even ethnic orientation cannot form a basis for a universal ethical argument.
B. Chicken soup or even Jewish humour (culture) does not make an ideological, ethical or political argument.

It was Moses Mendelssohn, an 18th century Jewish 'progressive' scholar, who coined the famous *Haskalah* (Jewish Enlightenment) insight: 'Be a Jew at Home and a *Goy* on the Street'. Mendelssohn's revelation for the modern Jew doesn't leave much room for doubt. Rather than encouraging the modern Jew to genuinely assimilate into a homogenous authentic universal ethos of equality, the *Haskalah* Jew is destined to live in a dual, deceptive mode, if not practically a state of schizophrenia. He is split between the solitary pleasure of a cosy, homely Jewish identity and the public appearance of the surrounding reality. The *Haskalah* Jew is deceiving his or her God when at home, and misleading the *Goy* once in the street.

In fact, it is this duality of tribalism and universalism that is at the very heart of the collective secular Jewish identity. This duality has never been properly resolved. Instead of redeeming the Jews it imposes a certain level of dishonesty.

A few attempts have been made to brush it off but they have all failed. Zionism for instance, offered to abolish the 'abnormal' condition of the 'Jewish Diaspora', in other words, it suggested that in a 'Jewish State' (intended as being for Jews Only) the differences between the 'home' and the 'street' would disappear. Though it managed to do this, at least for a while, there is no trace of universalism in either the Zionist's 'street' or in his 'home'.

The carnage Israel left behind in Lebanon (2006) or Gaza (2008) doesn't leave much room for doubt – Israel doesn't really offer us any lessons in universal cosmopolitanism. Marxism also attempted to make people look equal. In other words, it promised to make all 'homes' and people look the same. This idea was very appealing to a few West European and many East European Jews who even formed the Bund, a Jewish Socialist Party. Marxism was indeed successful for a while, however, nowadays it is actually consumerism that makes us all look homogenous (iPod, coca-cola, jeans etc'). Clearly, there is not much to celebrate there either.

It is from within the failure of these two competing grand ideologies that the matrix of negation marched triumphantly. The search for a contemporary, collective, secular Jewish identity is a perplexing endeavour. Just as in Mendelssohn's time, it aims at integrating the opposing categories of tribalism and univer-salism. But this can never be achieved, and this is exactly where 'hate politics' starts to play its part.

If you don't know who you are, just find yourself an enemy. In other words, 'tell me who you hate and I will tell you who you are.'

Mendelssohn must have understood the intrinsic clash between the 'cosmopolitan man' and the 'Jewish home'. He must have realised that universalism and tribalism are opposing categories. Being trained as a rabbi, Mendelssohn offered a pragmatic and practical solution – but this solution led to false and deceptive behaviour. Either you pretend to be a cosmopolitan while in the street or you lie to your creator at your dwelling. This behavioural code, though being very pragmatic, happens to be non-ethical by definition. It is based on deception – both self-deception and deceiving the other.

As we know, it was Mendelssohn's insight that was the cause of many Germanic Jews eventually converting to Christianity or just departing from any connection with Jewish collectivism, Jewish life or culture. Ethically, at least, Mendelssohn's middle way between orthodoxy and modernity failed to provide an answer. The third category Jewish leftwing activist falls straight into Mendelssohn's trap. They try desperately and unsuccess-fully to bridge the gap between tribal commitment and the universal call. Like Mendelssohn, they are doomed to failure.

Chapter 7

The Dialectic of Negation

Here are some quotes that reveal what early Zionist ideologists thought of their brothers, the Diaspora Jews, those for whom they were developing a nationalist project based on a philosophy of racial ethnic identity:

'The Jew is a caricature of a normal, natural human being, both physically and spiritually. As an individual in society he revolts and throws off the harness of social obligations, knows no order nor discipline.' (*Our Shomer 'Weltanschauung', Hashomer Hatzair, December 1936, p.26. As cited by Lenni Brenner*[36])

'The fact is undeniable that the Jews, collectively, are unhealthy and neurotic. Those professional Jews who, wounded to the quick, indignantly deny this truth are the greatest enemies of their race, for they thereby lead them to search for false solutions, or at most palliatives.' *(Ben Frommer, The Significance of a Jewish State, Jewish Call, Shanghai, May 1935, p.10. As cited by Lenni Brenner*[37])

'The enterprising spirit of the Jew is irrepressible. He refuses to remain a proletarian. He will grab at the first opportunity to advance to a higher rung in the social ladder.' (*The Economic Development of the Jewish People, Ber Borochov, 1916*[38])

'The emancipated Jew is insecure in his relations with his fellow-beings, timid with strangers, suspicious even toward the secret feeling of his friends. His best powers are exhausted in the suppression, or at least in the difficult concealment of his own real character. For he fears that this character might be recognised as Jewish, and he has never the satisfaction of showing himself as he is, in all his thoughts and sentiments. He becomes an inner cripple, and externally unreal, and thereby always ridiculous and hateful to all higher-feeling men, as is everything that is unreal. All the better Jews in Western Europe groan under this, or seek for alleviation. They no longer possess the belief which gives the patience necessary to bear sufferings, because it sees in them the will of a punishing but not loving God.' *(Address at the First Zionist Congress, Max Nordau, 1897[39])*

Early Zionist ideologists were pretty outspoken when it came to the 'Diaspora' Jewry. Ber Borochov eloquently diagnosed the inherent Jewish non-proletarian tendencies. Max Nordau didn't spare words when confronting the intrinsic post-emancipated Jewish social incompetence. In the eyes of Hashomer Hatzair, the Diaspora Jew is nothing but a caricature and, for Ben Frommer, it is nothing less than neurosis we are dealing with. Yet, they were optimistic, they somehow believed that a 'new beginning' would cure the emancipated Jew of what seemed to some as a 'disgraceful' fate. They believed in a global Jewish 'homecoming', they were convinced that such an endeavour would heal the Jews of their inherent symptoms.

In an article published just after the first Zionist Congress (1897) Ahad Ha'Am, the most prominent Jewish polemist at the time, wrote '...the Congress meant this: that in order to escape from all these troubles [the Jewish anti-social symptoms as described by Nordau] it is necessary to establish a Jewish State.'[40]

Being inspired by 19th century ideologies such as Nationalism, Marxism, Early Romanticism, Darwinism and Life Philosophy *(Leben Philosophie)*, early Zionists preached for the emerging of the bond between the Jew and 'his' soil. Naively, they believed that the love of farming, agriculture and nature would turn the emancipated Jew into an ordinary, civilized human being. Early Zionists predicted that Zionism would create a new, authentic form of Jewish-ness, in which Jews would be entitled to love themselves for who they are rather than who they claim to be. While the socialists amongst them were talking about a new commitment to working class ideology (Berl Kazanelson, Borochov, A.D. Gordon), those on the right wing (Jabotinsky, Frommer) dreamed of a master race that would emerge and rule the land.

Both Right and Left truly believed that, due to their homecoming, Jews would be able to replace their 'traditional traits' with aspirations towards sameness. They genuinely believed that Zionism would turn Jews into 'people like all people'. Failing to understand that the premise was categorically flawed for 'other people' do not wish to be 'like other people'. In other words, as long as Jews insisted on being like 'all people' they would always fail to be themselves.

Just as early Zionists had never tried to disguise the extent of their prophetic dream, they also didn't make any efforts to conceal their contempt towards their 'Diaspora' Jewish brothers. In their emerging fantasy of national awakening, Jews would divorce from greed and money seeking as well as cosmopolitan tendencies. In their vision, Zion was there to transform the Jew into an ordinary organic human being. The move to Zion was there to fill the chasm created by emancipation. The settlement in Zion was there to give birth to a new man. A Jew who looks at himself with pride, a Jew who fills Jewish-ness with meaning. A Jew who is defined by positive qualities rather than by mere negation.

Emancipated, Assimilated and Zionist
When it comes to secular Jews, things get complicated. While

observant Jews can easily list a few measurable qualities they identify with, for instance they follow Judaism, they observe Jewish laws, they follow the Talmud, they follow Kosher dietary restrictions, etc., emancipated secular Jews have very little to offer in terms of positive characteristics to identify with. Once you ask a secular Jew what makes him into a Jew you may hear the following: 'I am not a Christian nor am I a Muslim.' OK then, but what is it that makes you into a Jew in particular? He may say, 'I am not just American, French or British. I am somehow different.' In fact, the so-called emancipated, assimilated or secular Jews would find it hard to list any particular positive quality that may identify them as Jews. Emancipated Jews are identified by negation - they are defined by the many things they are not.

This is exactly where Zionism interfered. It was there to set the Jews up in a project that aimed towards an authentic identification. Zionism was there to let the Jew think in terms of 'belonging'. Within the Zionist phantasmic reality, the generations of home-comers were there to declare: 'We are the new Jews, we are Israelis, we are human beings like all other human beings, we live on our land, the land of our forefathers. We speak Hebrew, the language of our ancestors, we eat the fruit and vegetables that we ourselves farmed on our soil.'

Zionism has failed for various reasons. Zionism could never have prevailed. It has been entangled with an endless list of sins from day one. Yet, as much as Zionism quickly established itself as a criminal practice, some of its criticism of the emancipated Diaspora Jewish identity is worth looking into. At the end of the day, the so-called emancipated Diaspora Jew is still defined by negation and this fact alone has very many grave implications.

The Politics of Negation

In order to grasp what Jewish Diaspora identity means in the

21st century, we'd better try to find out whether the notion of emancipated Jewish identity has changed at all since the early Zionists exposed its problematic character more than a century ago. How, for instance, does a 'Jewish Marxist' refer to his Jewishness.

During my years in Europe I have come across groups of people who call themselves 'Jews for Peace', 'Jews for Justice in Palestine', 'Jews Against Zionism', 'Jews for this' and 'Jews for that'. I have recently heard about 'Jews for Boycott of Israeli Goods'. Occasionally I end up asking myself what stands at the core of this ethnocentric, separatist, peace-loving endeavour. I may as well admit that though I have come across many German peace activists, I have never come across an 'Aryan Palestinian Solidarity', 'Aryan for Peace' group or even Caucasian Anti-War campaigners. It is somehow Jews and only Jews who engage in racially-orientated or ethno-centric peace and solidarity campaigning.

Borochov and Nordau provided us with a possible answer. In the seeking of a 'political identity', the emancipated Jew ends up succumbing to the dialectic of negation. His or her political identity is defined by what he or she isn't rather than by who he or she is. United as a group, they aren't Germans, they aren't British, they aren't Aryans, they aren't Muslims, they aren't just ordinary proletarians or even boring peace-lovers, they aren't just common, working class people. They are Jews because they aren't anything else. At a first glance it seems as if nothing is wrong in being defined by negation. Yet, a deeper critical glance into the notion of negation may reveal some of the devastating aspects of this form of emancipated dialectic.

Ethical thinking may be the first victim of the dialectic of negation. In order to think or judge ethically, genuine, authentic, organic thinking is of the essence. Emmanuel Kant's categorical imperative ('Act only according to that maxim whereby you can, at the same time, will that it should become a universal law') identifies ethical thinking with an orientation that sets one on a self-search for a 'universal' insight. Clearly, such a process involves thorough self-reflection. Negation, on the other hand, requires the opposite. It involves scouting and searching into others' praxis. Again, rather than understanding who you are, one invests some effort in differentiating oneself from the other and from the universal. Rather than listening to one's conscience and engage in an authentic ethical judgment, the negating subject sets his or her relationships with his or her surrounding environment, based on pragmatic and practical decision-making and exchange. At most, one may present a pretence of ethical thinking, but no more than that.

The Israelis take a special pride in the IDF's 'code of ethics' (a set of principles that define 'The IDF Spirit: Values and Basic Rules'). Israelis claim that the IDF is the only army in the world to possess an 'ethical code'. Asa Kasher, the Israeli philosopher behind the ethical code, must have skipped Kant's contribution to ethics. For Kant, ethics is a matter of judgment rather than an internalisation of a given moral 'code' or rules. The ethical being, according to Kant, is distinguished by his or her capacity to judge ethically. The ethical subject is engaged in a constant dynamic ethical exercise rather than a symbolic acceptance of a given rule.

Similarly, many political institutions are also fascinated by the '1948 Human Rights Declaration'. They seem to believe that it conveys an absolute 'universal ethical standard' that transcends beyond time and place. In fact, this is not necessarily the case. The 1948 declaration is a mere representation of a set of universal judgments made at a given time and place (10 December 1948, Paris) by a group of people. For the obvious reasons, it fails to provide answers to some different questions that arise as we proceed in time and live through some dramatic changes.

As opposed to the Kantian vision of ethical judgements being distinguished by openness, the Declaration is interpreted by some as a set of moral rules. As such, it impedes an authentic moral exercise. It is not surprising, therefore, that Neocon think-tanks, moral interventionists, Israeli lobbies and supporters of the war against Islam ground their argument in the declaration. It conveys an image of an ethical argument.

Looking at Israeli *Hasbara* (propaganda), as well as at Neocon politics around the world and especially in America and the UK, reveals the bitter truth of the matter. Neocons and *Hasbara* always present a seemingly 'ethical' argument. They employ what looks like a moral excuse in order to introduce a pretext for a war. As we know, the so-called 'only democracy in the Middle East' is also the one that has locked Palestine's vast populations behind walls and barbed wire for decades. Similarly, people like Wolfowitz and Perle dragged America and Britain into a futile criminal war in Iraq in the name of 'moral interventionism', 'democracy' and 'liberation'. Clearly the Palestinians and the Iraqis are paying a heavy price as victims of the politics of negation, politics that convey a deceitful image of righteousness by means of cloning. But the Palestinians and the Iraqis are not alone.

The Westerner subject who is stained with the crime of genocide is also a victim of the Western shift towards politics of negation. Rather than defining ourselves by who we are, we get accustomed to our politicians defining us by whom we suppose to hate: once it was the 'Nazi', then the 'Red', then it was the 'axis of evil' and now it is the 'Islamofascists'. The list is obviously open to changes.

More frightening is the fact that people who succumb to the dialectic of negation cannot engage in peace-making and recon-ciliation. The reason is simple: the notion of peace, reconciliation and harmony entails a collapse of the politics of negation. From the point of view of negation, reconciliation means elimination. Loving your neighbour may lead towards an identity loss. Needless to say that in the last centuries, millions of European and American Jews have chosen peace and total assimilation. They have divorced their Jewish identity and disappeared into the masses.

However, the fact that emancipated Jewish identity is defined by negation may also help us to realise why it is that emancipated Jews are so often part of political campaigns and revolutionary movements: those who are defined by negation are always against something. It could be the bourgeoisie, capitalism, colonialism, Palestinians, Iraq, Iran, Islam, the Goyim, human rights abuse, historic revisionism, Zionism and so forth. Seemingly, the journey between 'dialectic of negation' and 'politics of hate' is rather short.

Unconsciousness is the Discourse
of the Goyim

Chapter 8

One Hundred Years of Jewish Solitude

Zionism is no longer a young movement. It is more than one hundred and ten years since the first Zionist Congress was held (1897) and more than ninety years have passed since the Balfour Declaration (1917) was issued, a promise given by the British Government to Zionist leaders to create a 'national Jewish home' in Palestine. It's been over six decades since the formation of the Jewish State and the mass ethnic cleansing of the vast majority of the indigenous Palestinian population. Not only is Zionism no longer young, it is far from being a unified ideological movement. In fact, it is almost impossible to determine these very basic elements: what is Zionism aiming for, who is its leader? Is there a linear ideological continuum between the Israeli vision of Middle East interests and the architects behind the New American Century project? Is there a continuum between the crime carried out against the Palestinian people in Gaza in the name of the war on terror and the crime against the Iraqi people committed in the name of 'democracy'? It is also difficult to find a demarcation line between Jewish ideology and Zionism. We are dealing here with largely overlapping identities.

Earlier on I suggested that it is possible to grasp the subject of Zionism in terms of an organismus in which each of its elements contributes towards the maintenance of the entire system. Within the Zionist network there is no need for a lucid system of hegemony. In such a network, each element is complying with its role. And indeed the success of Zionism is that the whole is greater than the sum of its parts.

Throughout the years, Zionism has become an efficient

system that serves what the Zionists define as primary Jewish interests. Within the Zionist framework, the Israelis colonise Palestine and the Jewish Diaspora is there to mobilise lobbies by recruiting international support. The Neocons transform the American army into an Israeli mission force. Anti-Zionists of Jewish descent (and this may even include proud self-haters such as myself) are there to portray an image of ideological plurality and ethical concern.

However, within such a network even the so-called 'enemies of the Jewish people' have a clear role. Ahmadinejad is the current 'Hitler' and the rest of the so-called 'Islamofascists' are there to finish the 'Nazi Judeocide'. In other words, the Zionist vision is there to offer a conclusive and coherent insight into the issue of contemporary Jewish identity and Jewish affairs. Moreover, Zionism is there to offer a new 'world order', with the English-speaking empire as a world policing force and a defender of Jewish interests.

Though traditionally we tend to associate Zionism with a particular Jewish national aspiration, as well as a Jewish call for the return to Zion (Palestine), this is not necessarily the only viable historical or philosophical interpretation of the Zionist endeavour. I suggest that it makes far more sense to regard Zionism as a tribal Jewish preservation project. In other words, Zionism can be interpreted as a Jewish global movement that has as its aim the prevention of assimilation. It is there to stop the disappearance of world Jewry. Accordingly, Zionism should be seen as an amalgam of different philosophies specialising in different forms of tribal separatism, disengagement and segregation. It is there to infuse the third category identity with meaning.

Such an interpretation may throw some new light on the significant power of Global Zionism, the general support of world Jewry for the Israeli State. It may throw some light on the role of those sporadic, yet, extremely loud, Jewish voices which happen to oppose Zionism. Such a terminological shift into the notion of Zionism will emphasise an ideological continuum between Herzl's take on assimilation and the late Sharon's 'unilateral disengagement', yet it will also expose a very embarrassing continuum between hard-core right-wing Zionism and the so-called Jewish left and Jewish anti-Zionism.

Leaving God Behind

Jews, like anyone else, are entitled to dump God, to leave their faith and to divorce from religion. Yet, dropping God is neither a philosophical argument nor a form of ethical reasoning. To abandon religion doesn't necessarily mean becoming a humanist and secularization doesn't imply universalism or any other ethical stand. Not only is dismissing the concept of God not a philosophy, it is not even an argument. It is mere practice. In fact, to replace God with an anthropocentric moral argument is what secularisation is all about.

Historically, it was Spinoza who launched the modernist attack on Judaic Biblical orthodoxy. Spinoza's goal was to replace the God of Abraham with reason. While Pre-WW2 Jewish intellectuals, such as Franz Rosenzweig[41], Herman Cohen[42], Gershom Scholem[43] and others, were trying to engage Spinoza's chasm by applying philosophical argument, post-WW2 Jewish philosophical confrontation with modernity has been replaced by a shallow form of Left identity politics and Zionist praxis.

A truly interesting text was published a few years ago by the London Jewish Chronicle (JC). It is a glimpse into the political and philosophical mantra of a Jewish, socialist as well as anti-Zionist couple who have rejected the God of Abraham. In spite of the fact that they are proud they have dumped God, they still hold a Seder (Passover dinner) and they circumcised their twin sons. They also gave them a 'faith-free' Bar Mitzvah. To a certain extent, the JC article is a dialogue between the voice of the mainstream 'Jewish community' and the so-called 'Jewish dissident voice'. This is the story of journalist Julia Bard (56) and teacher David Rosenberg (48), both founding members of the British Jewish Socialists. It is a peep into the strange and inconsistent world of the Jewish tribal left. I admit that it was Bard who opened my eyes and led me to a terminological shift that presents Zionism in a new light.

According to the JC: 'Julia Bard and David Rosenberg are committed Jews. They feel passionately about Jewish history, they have a strong Jewish element to their social lives and their children have inherited a love of Hebrew and Yiddish culture... David and Julia do not belong to a synagogue, do not believe in God and are antagonistic towards Zionism. They feel strongly that these factors should not exclude them from full acceptance as part of the mainstream Jewish community.'

Like many modern assimilated Jews, David and Julia insist on reducing Jewish-ness to a form of tribal orientation spiced up with some cultural aspects. They love Yiddish and they love 'Jewish History'. Very much like modern assimilated Jews and Israelis they probably regard the Bible as an exoteric historical text rather than an esoteric spiritual guideline. This isn't a crime.

Although David and Julia do not like God that much and in spite of the fact that they are not that impressed with Judaism, they still followed the Judaic blood ritual and had their children's foreskins removed. In spite of Julia and David's dismissal of the Jewish faith, they still very much want to be part of the Jewish community. I wonder why? What is it that they need from the Jewish community? Why don't they just 'get on' with their 'socialist agenda' and join the human family as ordinary people? Many people around the world do not believe in God, many millions of Westerners left their faith, yet, they do not insist on calling themselves Catholics, Hindus, Protestants or Muslims. They just go forth into new life in a multi-cultural, multi-faith society.

Julia believes in multi-culturalism, hence she answers: 'I

wanted to remain Jewish.... I want to prove that there is a way of being Jewish that doesn't involve saying prayers to a God you don't believe in.'

Apparently Julia, like many other emancipated Jews, is craving an authentic identity. She is looking for her individual secular voice while maintaining her ties with her Jewish heritage. Again this is not a crime, however, I wonder why she can't just regard herself as a Jew or even a secular Jew without appealing for 'acceptance' by the 'Jewish community'? For instance, I regard myself a 'Hebrew-speaking Palestinian', I do not seek anyone's approval to do so. I also regard myself as a 'proud, self-hating Jew' and again, I do not need anyone's approval. Julia, on the other hand, needs approval. Julia expects the Jewish community to accept her in spite of the fact that she rejects God and the faith of Judaism.

Julia suggests an answer, she says: 'I understand my Jewish identity as an ethnic identity...'

Perhaps we are getting somewhere. The magic words 'ethnicity' and 'identity', have been introduced into the discourse. What does Julia mean when she refers to 'ethnic identity'? Is it the famous old chicken soup or is it *Gefilte Fish*[44] this time? Is 'Jewish ethnic identity' a form of belonging to Jewish history and heritage? Again, I am pretty sure that no one is going to stop Julia and David from cheering themselves up by reading chapters of Jewish history, an endless chain of catastrophes. In fact no one is going to stop Julia and David from celebrating any of their cultural symptoms. Nevertheless, Julia and David want a bit more than mere celebration, they clearly want recognition.

Again I find myself slightly bewildered. Recognition is something you may aim to achieve, nevertheless, it isn't something you can ever demand. Among my sins I play jazz. I indeed want to be widely recognized as a leading saxophonist and an original voice, yet I would never consider insisting in a jazz magazine that the jazz community should accept me or acknowledge my contribution regardless of my merits. My 'acceptance' as an artist is obviously subject to my achievement and contribution to the art form. Julia insists upon being recognised as a Jew, without suggesting or specifying what her exact contribution to the Jewish discourse and experience is.

Seemingly, it is *identity* rather than reason that the JC and Bard are concerned with. Yet, it is clear that Bard believes that one's identity reflects upon one's authenticity. Bard, like many others, is obviously wrong. As explained earlier on, it is actually the other way around. Identity and identity-politics alienate one from any notion of authenticity. Identity politics aims at setting measures of identification, categories of belonging, it demands recognition. It prefers gathering and grouping rather than meditation on the self or any form of true reflection. In fact, people who possess a genuine notion of a self do not crave the acceptance of any community, whether Jewish or other. They are recognised for 'who they are' rather than accepted for what they claim to be.

Regarding herself as a 'progressive' Jew, Bard believes that 'Jewish future rests on the community being inclusive rather than exclusive.'[45] Being part of an ethnic collective, Julia is truly concerned with issues having to do with assimilation and preservation of the Jewish people. Yet, unlike the rabbinical institutes, she welcomes a hybridisation of a Jewish collective rather than a rigid uniformity. 'Those people who are bleating on about the Jewish community shrinking base it on a false assumption – that Judaism remains unchanging and that you can't be Jewish without being religious.'[46]

But there is a far greater concern raised by Bard. Seemingly, a 'liberated' Jew is disturbed by the fact that the Jewish community is 'shrinking'. One may wonder why a liberated being, a 'progressive' Jew and a 'socialist', is concerned with issues to do with assimilation and the disintegration of a 'reactionary' tribal and racially-oriented community.

The notion of Jewish Socialism may provide the answer. Jewish Socialism, like Judaism, is a unique, esoteric ideology that is primarily concerned with Jewish interests and Jewish-ness in general. This is what I found on the 'Who We Are' web page that the Jewish Socialist couple are associated with: 'We (Jewish Socialists' Groups) unite on issues we recognise as crucial for the future of the Jewish community.' Seemingly, Julia Bard and her Jewish *comrades* are part of the Jewish community, and the subjects they are concerned with are issues to do with the future of the Jewish tribe. Reading these lines rings a bell. It was actually my grandfather, the right-wing, racist *Irgun* commander terrorist, who insisted that 'Jewish Socialism' is not only inconsistent, it is deceitful to the bone.

The ordinary Marxist may wonder why Julia Bard, David Rosenberg and their comrades echo the words uttered by ultra-Zionist Israeli PM Golda Meir in the 1970s. 'To me,' says Meir, 'being Jewish means and has always meant being proud to be part of a people that has maintained its distinct identity for more than 2,000 years, with all the pain and torment that has been inflicted upon it.' (Golda Meir, My Life). Meir was also known for suggesting that mixed marriages were the biggest threat to the Jewish people. Like Bard, Meir was concerned with identity politics. Like Bard, Meir was a club member. Like Bard, Meir was worried about assimilation which she regarded as the 'greatest threat to the Jewish future'.

Could it be that Julia Bard and Golda Meir are two sides of the Zionist coin? Surely there is one clear difference? While Meir was an authentic hawk, she spoke tribal and thought tribal, Bard and friends speak 'universal' but it seems to me that they think tribal.

Zionism Revisited

Bard, Rosenberg and Meir are not being particularly innovative here, each demonstrating Zionism's original basic intent: to confront assimilation and the disintegration of Jewish identity.

Already in 1897, Herzl and Nordau had raised very similar concerns to those expressed by Meir and Bard.

If we redefine Zionism as a modern form of Jewish activism that aims to halt assimilation, we can then reassess all Jewish tribal activity as an internal debate within a diverse Zionist political movement – the colonising of Palestine can then be considered as just another one of the faces of Zionism. Jewish socialism and Jewish progressive activism fit very nicely into the Zionist project. As integral parts of the Zionist network, they are concerned with the future of the Jewish secular tribe – they are there to collect the lost souls amongst the humanist Jews, to bring them home for Hanukkah. The Israel lobby and the Alan Dershowitzes[47] of the world are the voices of Zionism; the third-category socialists are there to stop proud, self-hating Jews from blowing the whistle.

Are Bard, Rosenberg and comrades aware of what could be seen as their Zionist role? Do they consciously act on behalf of an abstract tribal network, or a 'Jewish conspiracy'? I do not think so. As I have said earlier, I do not believe in Jewish conspiracies: everything is done in the open. I also do not believe that so-called 'progressive' Jews are aware of the grand tribal project in which they participate so enthusiastically. Then again, most Israelis themselves are not fully aware of the larger scope of the Zionist project they serve, including the IDF soldiers manning the roadblocks in the Occupied Territories and even the pilots who drop bombs on densely-populated Gaza neighbourhoods. It may even be possible that the likes of Wolfowitz and Sharon and Netanyahu fail to understand their roles.

Zionism is so successful because it is a global project with no head and a lot of hands. It sets out a modern framework or even template for Jewish tribalism by incorporating all elements into a dynamic power, and transforms its opposition into a productive force.

Peace, *Shalom* and the Ghetto

Ariel Sharon, a man who spent the better part of his life killing the enemies of Israel, who made warmongering into an art form, suddenly changed his spots in June 2004. During what proved to be his very last days in power, Sharon became a *shalom*-lover, a Zionist dove – this master of blood politics suddenly introduced an initiative known as 'unilateral disengagement'.

Shalom is a rather confusing word, which doesn't necessarily translate as 'peace'. In its contemporary Hebrew sense, it refers to the conditions required to guarantee the security of the Jewish people in Israel. When official Israeli spokesmen refer to *shalom*, they somehow always end up talking about safety of one people only, the Jews.

Sharon, the old, tired soldier, realised that the best strategy for securing the future of the Jews-only state was to withdraw the relatively few Jewish settlers from the primarily Palestinian-populated area of Gaza and the northern West Bank, and to advocate a moderate version of Jewish national expansionism. Sharon understood that, although Israel has at its disposal all kinds of weaponry – conventional and nuclear, plus other WMDs – the Palestinians have but one: the demographic bomb. Indeed, Palestinians now make up the majority population between the Jordan River and the Mediterranean Sea.

As expected, Sharon's initiative was totally rejected by the hawks of his right-wing Likud Party. He didn't waste any time, however. He left his political home of more than three decades in 2005 and formed Kadima ('Forward'), a new party that advocated an immediate, unilateral, partial evacuation of the Occupied Territories. Israeli voters saluted the old general at the polls in the 2006 election, in which Kadima came first. They had evidently concurred with Sharon's ingenious political move, and the new party's rivals disappeared, at least temporarily.

Liberal democracy fulfils its promise once the voters' will is reflected in state affairs. The late Sharon had managed to pluck the right strings, invoking Jewish nostalgic yearning for the ghetto. He promised to erect a monumental barrier that would keep the Palestinians out. Sharon understood Nordau's genuine yearning for the *shtetl* better than any of his contemporaries. Zionism can be considered a rereading of the ghetto narrative in glamorous, positive terms. The ghetto, says Nordau, 'was, for the Jew of the past, not a prison but a refuge … In the ghetto, the Jew had his own world; it was the sure refuge which had, for him, the spiritual and moral value of a parental home.'[48]

Sharon had grasped Nordau's message of Jewish craving: Zionism is all about the abolition of the other, the re-creation of conditions in which Jews can celebrate their symptoms, in which they can love themselves for who they are – or, at least, who they *think* they are.

Sharon promised a barrier. Yet there was a serious dialectical chasm opening up. As much as Zionism promises to replace assimilation with a newly-made framework of detachment and isolation, it also promises to create an enlightened, humanist Jew who is entirely different from his Diaspora brethren. As much as Zionist Jews want to be protected by walls and by the nuclear deterrent, they also want to be 'citizens of the world'. The Israeli, too, wants to fly cheaply with Easyjet, eat *hummus* in Edgware Road on Christmas Eve, and make it early enough to be the first at the Oxford Street sales on Boxing Day. In short, the Israeli wants the impossible. Not bad for such a young national identity!

Zionism as a movement can be described theoretically as a dialectical struggle between the tribal praxis that aims for insularity, and the universal promise of openness and tolerance. It is an ongoing debate between Jerusalem and Athens, that tries to promise both, but it is doomed to failure because tribalism and universalism are like oil and water, they don't mix well. Jews who are subject to this schizophrenic ideology find themselves bouncing between two conflicting promises. As much as they insist on loving themselves for who they think they are, they hate themselves for what they happen to be. Such circumstances may be seen as the ultimate tragedy, a metaphysical limbo; nevertheless, it can be a powerful position.

As it happened, Sharon didn't make it to the polls. A stroke in 2005 left him in a permanent vegetative state, and Ehud Olmert took his place. A few weeks later, Olmert won the election, though not as easily as Sharon would have done. He formed a centrist national unity government with the Labour Party and created the necessary political atmosphere in which to implement Sharon's unilateral agenda. But then the inevitable happened. As soon as there was a relatively minor incident involving Hizbullah on the Lebanese side of Israel's northern border, Olmert – with the support of his *shalom*-seeking 'centrist unity government' – unleashed Israeli military might and flattened Lebanon's infrastructure. It bears mentioning that Olmert's aggression was actually the natural continuation of Sharon's *shalom* initiative, the embodiment of the general's ghetto philosophy. (The new Jewish ghetto, though, resembles a hostile fortress with enough nuclear firepower to turn the Middle East into dust.)

Once hostilities had commenced, the Israelis – who, just a few months earlier, were blessing Sharon for his 'peace' initiative – succumbed to the usual heroic spirit of flames and death. As soon as the war started, they rallied in support of their government, amongst them, of course, the intellectual left. Veteran Israeli peace activist and journalist Uri Avnery wrote: 'When the government started this war, an impressive line-up of writers supported it. Amos Oz, A. B. Yehoshua and David Grossman, who regularly appear as a political trio, were united again in their support of the government and used all their considerable verbal talents to justify the war. They were not satisfied with that: some days after the beginning of the war, the three published a joint ad in the papers, expressing their enthusiastic backing for the operation.'[49]

The Israeli 2006 military campaign in Lebanon was not a great success – it was, in fact, a total disaster. The Israeli army failed. Hizbullah rockets rained down on northern Israel. Israeli cities north of Hadera turned into ghost towns. It didn't take long before Oz, Yehoshua and Grossman changed their minds. Teased Avnery: 'Some people are now pretending that this group was really against the war. To whit [sic]: some days before the end they published a second tripartite ad, this time calling for its termination. At the same time, Meretz and Peace Now [activist groups with which Oz is affiliated] also changed course. But not one of them apologised or showed remorse for their prior support for the killing and destruction. Their new position was: the war was indeed very good, but now the time has come to put an end to it.'[50]

Not only did the Israeli left change its mind, the entire Israeli public turned against its leadership: Olmert's popularity dropped sharply. Labour Defence Minister Amir Peretz's political career became a subject matter for historians only. IDF generals were mocked in the media.

Frequent changes of this sort in the mood of the Israeli public are another outcome of Zionist collective neurosis. Yet again, they love themselves for who they think they are, but nevertheless hate themselves for what they happen to be.

Chapter 9

Jewish Unconsciousness is the Discourse of the *Goyim*

What Zionists think of themselves is not very interesting; far more intriguing is the duality referred to above, the chasm between who they think they are and what they actually are, between self-image and public image, consciousness and unconsciousness. Unconsciousness, says Lacan, is the 'discourse of the other', which is very much the male fear of impotence. Rather than the anxiety induced by the fear of being caught malfunctioning, it is the fear of being known as dysfunctional. The real terror here is the unbearable threat that the fiasco may become public knowledge.

At the time of the 2006 Lebanon war, the Israelis' 'discourse of the other' encompassed CNN, Sky TV, BBC and the West in general. As the war proceeded, it began to appear as though resentment was mounting amongst those who were no longer willing to accept Israeli brutality. Indeed, this gulf between the confident Israeli self-image and the total contempt of the other is exactly where the neurosis of Yehoshua, Oz, Grossman and the majority of Israelis came into play.

Two and half years after its military flop in Lebanon, Israel found itself once again in the midst of a second disastrous war that it had launched. This was Operation Cast Lead (2008), a total war against the people of Gaza and their democratically-elected leadership, Hamas. Along the campaign, Israel attempted to implement the lesson of the 2006 war. I think, probably optimistically, that by then, somebody at the state *hasbara* bureau must have read Lacan. The Israelis would try to save themselves from fully grasping who they are and what they do by blocking out every possible mirror. Consequently the IDF barred all foreign media from entering Gaza, in order to guarantee a propaganda success. It wasn't just about barring *Goyim* from entering the battle zone, but about preventing Israelis and Zionist Jews around the world from seeing themselves through the gaze of the *Goyim*. It was a crude attempt to divert the discourse so that Jewish unconsciousness was kept intact.

As one might expect, this approach was completely counter-effective. While the Western media outlets were happy to obey Israel's demand for media blackout, the Arab and Iranian news networks were committed to the principle of news coverage.

At one point during the war, Al-Jazeera and Iran's Press TV became the only source of live feed from the battlefield. In Lacanian terms, not only had the truth of Israeli atrocities become the discourse of the *Goyim*, but it was directly fuelled and maintained by the 'ultimate enemy': the Israelis ended up seeing themselves through the gaze of Arabs, Iranians, *Muslims*. This must have been a painful experience.

Night after night we saw Israeli spokesmen denying the use of WMD, while behind their backs every foreign TV network projected live images of white phosphorus bursting over Gaza's neighbourhoods. Humiliated and pulverised, Israelis saw their true nature exposed.

A Serious Man

The reading of Jewish unconsciousness as the discourse of the *Goyim* is key to understanding Jewish political activism, Jewish collectivism in general and tribal collective schizophrenia. 'It doesn't matter what the *goyim* say, but rather what the Jews do,' is one of Ben-Gurion's famous axioms; in practice, however, as far as the Jewish unconscious is concerned, what really matters is what the *Goyim* see and think, but are reluctant to say.

The Coen Brothers' 2009 film *A Serious Man* explores this theme in a sharp, profound manner. A cinematic allegory of

Jewish cultural detachment, *A Serious Man* is a masterpiece that elaborates on the abnormalities of Jewish tribal existence. It does not explicitly touch upon issues related to Israel, Zionism, the occupation or anything directly linked to the Jewish state. Instead, it reflects on Jewish Diaspora life, Jewish segregation and the misery of operating within the Judeo-centric tribal template. It has much to say about Jewish alienation. At the same time, *A Serious Man* delivers a clear message regarding Israel and Zionism, for Israel is the Jewish state and, despite the Zionist promise to build a civilised nation, it functions as a Jewish ghetto, subject to all the symptoms of abnormality conveyed by the Coens.

Set in Minneapolis in 1967 – without a doubt a very signif-icant year in Jewish history – *A Serious Man* tells the story of Larry, a Jewish physics professor and a family man. In just two hours, we watch as Larry's life collapses. His disastrous existence is a glimpse into the tribally segregated society with which he is inherently associated.

Larry's dream-life plays an important role in the film. In a dream, he meets his true nature, his fears, his desires and his unethical self. While in waking life Larry is a castrated, dysfunc-tional family man, in his dream he somehow overcomes his weaknesses. He makes love to his neighbour, a friendly, stoned woman; he brings his troubled brother to the river and fearlessly sends him to Canada in a canoe, giving him money (a bribe that had been given to Larry earlier) for a fresh start. Yet in the same dream, both he and his brother are punished immediately; his anti-Semitic neighbour hunts Larry with a rifle normally reserved for shooting animals. 'Kill the Jew,' the *Goy* orders his son. At this point, Larry wakes up.

In the dream, Larry is confronted with his guilt through his *Goy* neighbour. Rather than the fear of being unethical, it is the fear of being *caught out* as unethical that torments Larry. It is the 'discourse of the other' (the gun-toting neighbour) that introduces Larry unconsciously to a sense of guilt. I link this back to the case of Israel: it is not the idea of being unethical that torments Israelis and their supporters, but the idea of being *'caught out'* as such.

A Serious Man opens with a quote after the medieval French rabbi and Biblical scholar Rashi: 'Receive with simplicity everything that happens to you.' Rashi's eloquent words echo the *Book of Job,* which is generally considered an attempt to reconcile the existence of God with evil. Such an attempt was very common amongst Jews of all religious degrees after the Holocaust, as they repeatedly asked how, if God exists, could he permit Auschwitz to happen. To a certain extent, Larry asks his local rabbis a similar question: 'What is *Hashem* [God] trying to tell me?' The rabbis cannot offer any answer. Like the *Book of Job* and Rashi, they have nothing concrete to suggest other than 'acceptance'. The rabbis are there to spin, to convey a pretence of reason. They are there to cover a black hole. They cannot reconcile God with evil in the world, nor can they explain Jewish suffering.

Interestingly, the Coens present an answer of their own, which has nothing to do with *Hashem.* For them, it is actually the abnormal culture inherent in the 'Jewish ghetto' mindset that is the root cause of Jewish suffering. While, in the film, it is the *Goy* neighbour who initially leads Larry to face his guilt through contempt, in reality it is the *goy* spectator who is being exposed to the secret Jewish inner life via Hollywood and the big screen. Thanks to the Coens, we are confronted with that which the Jews would prefer to disguise; to a certain extent, the filmmakers adopt the whistleblower role. They bring to light a cinematic interpretation of the Lacanian discourse of the other. The Coens' Jewish tribal cinematic reality is the Jewish unconscious, of which Jews are far from being proud. Like Al-Jazeera and Press TV in Gaza, the Coens reveal Jewish ghetto malaise to an audience of millions. But they also tackle the notion of Jewish unconsciousness by the means of mirroring.

Chapter 10

The Righteous Jew

I believe the sudden change in the Israeli collective mood, after the 2006 Lebanon war, was the outcome of an attempt to resolve the schizophrenic state of being tangled up with Zionism. The conflict between the tribal and the universal ripened into a state of colossal phobia. The Israeli leading writers Oz, Yehoshua and Grossman were practically bouncing between these extremes, between the insularity of Jerusalem and the openness of Athens, between the repellent *shtetl* and the glamorous metropolis.

The pattern is clear: the more Israelis want to secure themselves by clinging to isolation, the more death they spread around themselves. Once again, this reading of Israeli reality can help us to understand the magnitude of Operation Cast Lead, the 2008–09 Gaza assault, and the excessive use of power in that conflict. The more Israel wanted to justify Sharon's unilateral withdrawal from Gaza, the more corpses they had to leave behind only a few years later. Nor was this merely a political matter – as much as 94 percent of the Israeli Jewish population supported the lethal measures taken by the IDF against Palestinian civilians in Gaza[51]. But herein lies a problem. The more death the Israelis cause, the less they feel that they resemble the rest of humanity, and the more they begin to hate the leaders who had set them on such a chaotic path.

Israelis perceive themselves as inhabiting a democracy, and indeed Israel is a democracy, albeit a racially-selective and exclusive one. Olmert's 2006 reprisal in Lebanon reflected the wishes of the majority, at least at the beginning of the war. The emerging Israeli dissatisfaction with Olmert, Peretz and the IDF revealed a severe conflict within the Israeli collective psyche. The people ended up hating Olmert and company but it is in fact themselves they can no longer stand. The more Israelis detest themselves, the more horrified they become at their doomed situation. They despise the fact that they might have lost the ghetto for good, yet have failed to join the community of nations. They have never become 'people like all people'. To repeat: the more they insist on loving themselves for who they think they are, the more they loathe themselves for what they have become.

Is the case of the Jewish anti-Zionists Bard and Rosenberg any different? Aren't they falling into the exact same trap? Don't they love themselves for being enlightened, progressive socialists, while at the same time sinking into neurosis upon realising that being Jewish tribal *petit bourgeois*, they have never managed to join the human family, let alone the working class? Like the Israelis, Bard and Rosenberg and, generally speaking, all 'righteous Jews' who operate within 'Jews only' political clubs have failed to find a way to merge Athens and Jerusalem. It may as well be possible that Athens and Jerusalem can never be blended together into a lucid and coherent political world view.

I guess that three escape routes are left for Zionists – and the third category Jews:

1. *Total segregation.* This form of Zionism eliminates the notion of the other, or any correspondence or exchange with such an other. Such a solution is reflected in Sharon's disengagement as well as in the Jewish socialists clinging to tribalism and anti-assimilationism. The current Netanyahu government has adopted this route, consciously and willingly steering Israeli international affairs toward conflict.

2. *Return to orthodoxy.* The numbers of Israelis leaving behind secular Jewish culture to re-embrace the observance of religious Judaism reveal that this solution is, in fact,

becoming a common choice. In 2007 the Israel Democratic Institute (IDI) demographic survey found that the percentage of Jews describing themselves as secular has dropped sharply over the past 30 years, while the religious and traditional proportions had risen. The annual survey found that the secular public comprised only 20% of the Israeli population - compared to 41% in 1974[52].

3. *Flight from Jewish-ness.* Departing from Jewish-ness, Jerusalem and any other form of Judaic tribalism, and leaving 'Chosen-ness' behind. This is probably the only form of genuine secular Jewish resistance to Zionism one can take seriously.

Nordau, no doubt a clever man, could identify the new Marranos, the Jews who split from Judaism, with real conviction, as the greatest danger for a tribal Jewish future. Like the other anti-assimilationists, Nordau was very explicit about it: 'Many try to save themselves by flight from Judaism. But racial anti-Semitism denies the power of change by baptism, and this mode of salvation does not seem to have much prospect ... In this way there arises a new Marrano, who is worse than the old. The latter had an idealistic direction – a secret desire for truth or a heart-breaking distress of conscience, and they often sought for pardon and purification through Martyrdom.'

Nordau had already realised in 1897 that the new Marranos, who genuinely craved truth and could even manage to find it outside the *shtetl*, constituted the ultimate danger. Nevertheless, he was living in a world inflamed with Darwinism and biological determinism. Nowadays, biological determinism is – hopefully – behind us, and people are free to escape their so-called 'fate'. Nowadays, hardly anyone thinks in terms of blood, except Zionists, Israelis, and, embarrassingly enough, some of the so-called Jewish 'socialists'.

To be a Zionist is to prevent assimilation, to stop Jews from 'drifting away', to engage in some form of Judeo-centric political discourse. Zionism, as we know it, indeed colonises Palestine, but its branches are far-reaching. It is not a local movement supported by some enthusiastic lobbies around the world, but a global matrix that possesses the capacity to shape and reshape the notion of the Jewish ghetto, to form and re-form the dialectic of Chosen-ness, to balance the emerging tension between insularity and openness yet to include most Jews. Zionism is a global network with no head, it is a spirit – spirit, unfortunately, cannot be defeated. Yet, it must be exposed for what it is.

Chapter 11

Sex and Anti Semitism

For the last decade I have been drawing many of my insights from a man who has been totally eradicated from Western academic and scholarly discourse. Considering the influence he exerted in the first half of the twentieth century, this complete disappearance certainly raises some questions. Wittgenstein considered him to have had a major impact on his life. James Joyce drew upon him when writing *Ulysses*. He inspired Robert Musil and Hermann Broch. One can easily trace his thoughts in Lacan and Heidegger. Freud was also interested in his ideas. Even Hitler supposedly mentioned him, admitting: 'There was one decent Jew, and he killed himself.' This man was Otto Weininger, and although he was one of the most influential thinkers of the first four decades of the twentieth century, few are still familiar with his thoughts or have even heard his name. Weininger was an anti-Semite as well as a radical misogynist. He didn't like Jews or women, yet, as you might have already suspected, he was a Jew himself and, insofar as historical research can disclose such truths, an effeminate one.

Weininger was an aphorism artist. Many of his statements can't be taken seriously. Some of his anti-woman and anti-Jewish rants evoke the image of a naughty schoolboy struggling to understand the concept of adulthood. Yet Weininger is an astonishing thinker. His understanding of the notion of genius could easily fit into the final section of Kant's third critique; his understanding of sexuality is overwhelmingly astute given that his book was published when he was just twenty-one years old. Many of Weininger's opponents happen to admit to the man's brilliant talent. Simply put, there is far too much wisdom in

Weininger for us to cast him aside without looking.

There is a personal side to my admiration: Weininger helped me grasp who I am, or rather who I may be, what I do, what I try to achieve and why my detractors invest so much effort trying to stop me.

Weininger published *Sex and Character*, his one and only book, in 1903. It was presented as a philosophical study of sexuality. A ferocious attack on the concept of femininity, it nevertheless isn't only women Weininger appears to despise – he presents Jews as degraded beings as well, and Englishmen as effeminate characters. Weininger is nothing less than outrageous. Some of my female associates who began reading the text dismissed it before they reached the end of the first paragraph. Yet I insist that almost every sentence in Weininger's book should be considered thought-provoking literature. Weininger hates almost everything that fails to be Aryan masculinity. His tendency toward mathematical formulation is slightly childish, and no doubt dated. He makes some categorical mistakes. At the same time, he induces deep ideological, essentialist and metaphysical thinking.

Weininger on Sexuality

Weininger's point of departure is far from original. Man and woman, he says, are merely types. In other words, the individual appearance is basically a manifestation of a mixture of the two types. Every individual is a compound of two sexual types in different proportions. Some men are more masculine than others, and some women are more feminine than their sisters. This idea is obviously supported by basic physiological observations as well as sophisticated genetic and biological study.

Weininger doesn't stop there, however. He moves on to formulate the 'law of sexual attraction': 'For true sexual union it is necessary that there come together a complete Male and a complete Female.'[53] The bond between a man and a woman results in a unity of maleness and femaleness to which the two partners mutually contribute. In practice, Weininger speaks here of the complementary between men and women. Each partner contributes toward the formation of a greater femininity and masculinity. If Tony is 55 percent male and 45 percent female, and Sue is 45 percent male and 55 percent female, the sum of their added maleness and femaleness results in a perfect unity of 100 percent male and 100 percent female. In other words, as far as sexual attraction is concerned, we can expect Tony and Sue to be highly excited about each other. Their union brings together a complete unity of man and woman. They also have a lot in common for Tony has a lot of woman in him and Sue, similarly, possesses a lot of man in her.

Needless to say, Weininger's reference to human beings as statistical objects is slightly bizarre as well as problematic. When we examine the people around us we do not see mathematical figures or clear-cut divisions between masculinity and femininity. We, instead, see desires, wishes, intentions, hopes and sexual needs. Yet Weininger's idea, regardless of its practical implications, is far from stupid. The idea that Tony and Sue are engaged in a complementary relationship is very explanatory. Tony is attracted to Sue not only for her feminine qualities, but because he finds in Sue his missing masculinity. Similarly, Sue celebrates the discovery of her lacking femininity. According to Weininger, we are most attracted to those who bring us closer to this unity.

Naturally, we would expect the bond between extreme masculinity and extreme femininity to result in a high degree of sexual attraction. However, as Weininger points out, this attraction is coupled with very little cross-gender understanding: 'The more femaleness a woman possess the less will she under-stand a man ... So also the more manly a man is the less will he understand women.'[54] The reasoning is clear: the more femaleness a woman possesses, the less maleness is present in her physical and psychological makeup. Assume, for example, that Mark is the ultimate macho man, 99 percent male, and Deborah is very feminine to a similar extent. Their sexual intensity might be explosive beyond belief, yet the quality of their communication beforehand or afterward will be nil. With 1 percent femininity, Mark can never understand Deborah, and vice versa. Mark will probably turn his back to Deborah as soon as the intercourse is over. He falls asleep and she ends up upset.

This idea is shocking in its simplicity, but its implications are powerful. It leaves the Left's discourse in ruins. For if Weininger is correct, comprehension of the other is conditioned by a form of self-realisation. The notion of empathy and otherness so enthusiastically embraced by the post-Second World War Left falls apart. If I can understand my beloved only inasmuch as I possess enough of her in me, it follows that we can only understand the other as long as we have enough of the other in us. This insight may explain why the Left, along with the entire discourse of multiculturalism, collapsed after the events of 11 September 2001. The lack of empathy with Arabs and Muslims amongst so-called 'progressive' liberals can be accounted for by the fact that they had very little Arab or Muslim in them, in fact, they may have very little in them except themselves.

Such a reading may explain why the Western Left failed to grasp the transformation within the Arab world. As much as the Left claims to support the Arab masses' uprising against their pro-American tyrants, it somehow found it hard to admit that what we see in the Arab World is not exactly a Socialist revolution. In Weiningerian terminology, the Left has failed to read the situation in the Arab world because it has very little in common with Arab culture. The Left was doomed to fail on that front.

The Genius and the Artist

This concept of possessing different psychological characteristics is further explored by Weininger in his treatment of the genius.

For him, it is obvious that the genius isn't merely a gifted being. Genius isn't talent, nor is it a quality that can be learned or developed. The genius is rather '... a man who discovers many others in himself. He is a man with many men in his personality. But then the genius can understand other men better than they can understand themselves, because within himself he has not only the character he is grasping, but also its opposite. Duality is necessary for observation and comprehension ... in short, to understand man means to have equal parts of himself and the opposite in one.'[55]

In a way, the genius is a person who hosts a dialectic dynamism that allows the rich prospects of the world to come alive. To a certain extent, Weininger hints here at the positive qualities of schizophrenia, ideas that were further explored by Lacan years later.

The genius is always telling us something about the world that we didn't know before. The scientist observes the material world, and the philosopher looks into the realm of ideas. The artist derives insight by looking into him or herself: 'In art, self-exploration is exploration of the world...'[56].

Weininger argues that the genius is a subject to the 'strangest passions' and 'most repulsive instincts', but that those passions are opposed by other internal characters. For example, 'Zola, who has so faithfully described the impulse to commit murder, didn't commit murder himself because there were so many other characters in him.'[57] Zola, according to Weininger, would recognise the murderous impulse better than the murderer himself, rather than merely being subject to it. The ability to persuasively depict a fictional character is attributable to the fact that the character and its oppositions are well-orientated within the artist's psyche.

Weininger's appeal, for me, has much to do with this idea. In my fictional writing I have given birth to some charming yet appalling Israeli protagonists, all of them doomed people speeding toward a concrete wall. I write about people who never manage to live with the terms they have imposed upon themselves, people who never find their way home. In my fiction one meets people who cannot escape their fate. In my political and ideological writing, I try to establish a philosophical pattern that can enlighten the complexity of Jewish-ness. I search for the metaphysical mechanisms that make Israel and the Jewish world so *different*. In my early days I believed myself to be an autonomous thinker, positing himself in a detached, Archimedean surveying position. Thanks to Weininger, I realised how wrong I was – I was not detached from the reality about which I wrote, and I never shall be. I am not looking at the Jews, or at Jewish identity, I am not looking at Israelis. I am actually looking in the mirror. With contempt, I am actually elaborating on the Jew in me.

The Jew in me is not an island. He is joined by hostile enemies and counter-personalities who have also settled in my psyche. There are, inside me, many characters that oppose each other. It isn't as horrifying as it might sound. In fact, it is rather productive, amusing and certainly revealing.

The Anti-Semite

Following his own paradigm, Weininger argues: 'People love in others the qualities they would like to have but do not actually have in any great degree. So we only hate in others what we do not wish to be and what, notwithstanding, we are partly. We hate only qualities to which we approximate, but which we realise first in other persons … Thus the fact is explained that the bitterest anti-Semites are to be found amongst the Jews themselves.'[58]

According to Weininger, some Jews oppose in others that which they despise in themselves. This tendency is called anti-Semitism, but Jews are not alone. Some non-Jews find Jewish tendencies within themselves as well. Weininger elaborates:

'Even Richard Wagner, the bitterest anti-Semite, cannot be held free of accretion of Jewish-ness, even in his art.'[59] I would argue that, for Weininger, Jewish-ness isn't at all a racial category, but a mindset that some of us possess and a very few of us try to oppose.

Isn't that merely to repeat Marx's treatment of Jewish identity, explored in his famous essay 'On The Jewish Question'? Marx equates Jews with capitalism, self-interest and money-grubbing. For him, capitalism is Judaism, and Judaism is capitalism. The Jews have liberated themselves to the point where Christians have become Jews. He concludes ferociously: 'The social emancipation of the Jew is the emancipation of society from Judaism.'[60] Judging Marx's ideas in the Weiningerian frame of reference may suggest that Marx's analysis is the outcome of Marx being Jewish himself. In other words, Marxism is the outcome of Marx's capacity to oppose the Jew within.

As we can see, Weininger has provided us with a pretty useful analytical tool. He is granting us insight into the subject of hatred and self-hatred, going as far as arguing: 'The Aryan has to thank the Jew that through him, he knows to guard against Judaism as a possibility within himself.'[61] In other words, antagonism towards others can be grasped as a manifestation of self-contempt. Thus the Nazi hatred toward anything even remotely Jewish could also be explained as a form of hostility towards the Jew within.

But if hatred is, at least partly, a form of self-negation, I have to admit that my own personal war against Zionism and Jewish identity politics could be seen as a war I have declared against myself. Taking it a step further, we may all have to admit that fighting racism for real primarily entails opposing the racist within.

Otto Weininger was just twenty-three when he committed suicide. One may wonder how he knew so much about women. Why did he hate them so? How did he know so much about

Jews, and why did he hate *them* so? The answer can be elicited from Weininger's thoughts, though not from his own words. He hated women and Jews because he was a woman and a Jew. He adored Aryan masculinity because he probably lacked that quality in any significant amount in his own being. This revelation probably led Weininger to kill himself, just a month after the publication of his book. Very likely, he had managed to understand what his book was all about.

Chapter 12

Eretz Yisrael vs. *Galut*

For more than half a century, opponents of the Jewish State have identified Israel's policies with Zionism. Yet they may have been wrong to do so. Zionism does indeed dictate the plunder of Palestine in the name of Jewish national aspiration and 'home-coming'. Israel has been efficient in translating Zionist philosophy into brutal practice. However, Israelis – more precisely, the vast majority of Israeli-born secular Jews – are not motivated by Zionist ideology. Its spirit and symbols are virtually meaningless to them. Zionism is, for most of them, either an archaic notion or a foreign concept altogether. Most forms of 'anti-Zionism', then, have hardly any effect on Israel, Israeli politics or the Israelis themselves. Zionism is largely a Jewish Diaspora discourse.

Zionism vs. Israel

'I am a human being, I am a Jew and I am an Israeli. Zionism was an instrument to move me from the Jewish state of being to the Israeli state of being. I think it was Ben-Gurion who said that the Zionist movement was the scaffolding to build the home, and that after the state's establishment it should be dismantled.' *Avraham Burg*[62]

If Zionism exists to maintain Jewish entitlement to a national home in Zion, Israeli-born Jews live this reality from the start. For them, Zionism is a remote chapter of history associated with an old photograph of a man with a big black beard (Herzl). For Israelis, Zionism is not a transformation waiting to happen, but a tedious and dated body of ideas with little relevance whatsoever to their lives.

For the new Israelites, the *Galut* (Diaspora) has negative connotations. It is associated with ghettos, shame and persecution. However, this term is not used to refer to downtown Manhattan or London's Soho; contemporary Israelis do not identify their emigration from Israel as a return to the *Galut*. Like other migrant populations, they are only in search of a better life somewhere else. For most Israelis, their country is far from being a heroic, glorious place – after more than sixty years with the same spouse, they no longer appreciate her beauty.

Israeli-born secular Jews, the products of the Zionist transformation, are now so used to their existence in the region that they have lost their Jewish survival instincts. Instead they have adopted a hedonistic interpretation of Western enlightened individualism, which banishes the last remnants of tribal collectivism. This condition may explain why Israel was defeated in the 2006 Lebanon war. The new Israelis don't see any reason to sacrifice themselves on a collective Jewish altar. They are far more interested in exploring the pragmatic aspects of 'the good life'. Perhaps it is for this reason that the Israeli military didn't manage to subdue Hamas in Operation Cast Lead. In order to do so, Israeli generals would need to implement courageous ground tactics. They realise that carpet-bombing Gaza and dropping white phosphorus on UN shelters are likely to fail to produce the 'necessary results', yet there is nothing else they can do. Hedonistic societies do not produce Spartan warriors, and without real warriors at your disposal you're better off fighting from afar. Needless to say, the Palestinians, the Syrians, Hizbullah and the Iranians see it all. Day by day they analyse Israel's cowardly tactics, and properly interpret Israeli reality. They know Israel's days are numbered. Interestingly enough, the US military elite is also reviewing the situation – they have begun to grasp that Israel is no longer a strategic US asset.

On the face of it, Israelis do not seem that concerned with the emerging inevitability of their fate, at least not openly. Young Israelis are concerned largely with personal survival. They are escapists, asking: 'How the hell can I get out of here?' As soon as they complete their compulsory military duty, they either rush to Ben-Gurion Airport or learn how to switch off all the news channels. Israelis are leaving their homeland in growing numbers. Those doomed to stay behind belong to an apathetic culture of indifference.

Beaufort

Beaufort, an award-winning Israeli war film produced in 2007, is an astonishing exposure of Israeli fatigue and defeatism. It tells the story of an IDF special infantry unit, dug in at a Byzantine fortress atop a mountain in South Lebanon. The action takes place in 2000, days before the first Israeli withdrawal from Lebanon. The unit is surrounded by Hizbullah fighters. Day and night they live in trenches, hide in concrete shelters and are subject to unending barrages of mortar rounds and missiles. Though they all dream about their lives after returning from the hell in which they are caught, they die one after another at the hands of an unseen enemy.

Israeli audiences loved *Beaufort*. I believe they saw in it an allegory of their own terminal state. As much as the Israeli soldiers in the film long to run away as far as they can, whether that means settling in New York or getting stoned in Goa, Israeli society is coming to terms with the country's temporality and futile existence. Like the soldiers, Israelis want to become New Yorkers, Parisians, Londoners and Berliners (apparently even the number of Israelis queuing for Polish passports is increasing daily). *Beaufort* evokes a society under siege, the realisation that there may be no escape routes left, whether in physical terms or as a result of growing indifference. Time is running out.

Israel In The Eyes of The Diaspora

Although, like the soldiers in *Beaufort*, the people of Sderot or Ashkelon are happy to leave everything behind and run for their lives, for many Diaspora Jews Israel represents nothing less than a lucid model of glory. For them it is both 'meaning' as well as 'meaning in the making', the symbolic liberation and redemption of Jewish misery. Israel, to them, is everything the Diaspora Jew is not: it is full of *chutzpah*, forceful, militant, standing up for what it believes in. Accordingly, for a young Jew from Golders Green or Brooklyn, making *aliyah*[63] or joining what he or she mistakenly regards as the heroic Israeli army is far more glorious than joining Dad's law or accounting firm or dental practice. Though the majority of young Diaspora Jews choose to get on with their lives in their native countries and avoid 'taking advantage' of the Zionist challenge to make *aliyah*, Zionism still provides them with a symbolic identifier.

Few Jewish parents would stop their son or daughter from joining the IDF. Why should they, after all? It's a very safe army to be in; it avoids ground battle and kills from afar. Every Jewish father in the Diaspora must accept that it may be useful for his youngster to learn how to drive a tank, fly a helicopter or shoot an MK-47. Unlike the shockingly under-equipped Palestinian warriors who die stopping *Merkava* tanks with their bodies, Israeli soldiers barely ever risk their lives. Making heroic *aliyah* and joining the IDF seems to be a relatively safe adventure, at least for the time being.

Wandering Around

Zionism 'invented' the Jewish nation, ushering its national home, Israel, into a conflict that is now assuming global proportions and becoming a serious global threat. Yet, as I have noted, for the Israelis in the eye of the storm, 'Zionism' means very little. They enthusiastically join the IDF not because they are Zionists, but because they are Jews . The notion of the 'wandering Jew' thus has a new meaning. The dialectic between the Diaspora and *Eretz Yisrael* consists of a flow and counter-flow of yearning, aspiration and migration. Diaspora Jews are inspired by the Zionist fantasy of Israel; Israeli Jews, on the other hand, are determined to escape their increasingly besieged lives. The Diaspora is heading toward Israel at the same time as desperate Israeli Jews aspire toward getting out. There is, then, a dialectic tension between Diaspora Jewish identity and Israeli-ness, which is largely related to the Zionist project. Zionism and Israel are two diverse poles that together inform contemporary Jewish experience.

Love Yourself as Much as You Hate Everyone Else

Unlike the Western Diaspora secular Jew, who struggles to establish a coherent continuum between Chosen-ness and a multi-ethnic open society, Israel permits a coherent and consistent symbolic interpretation of tribal supremacism, in which 'love yourself as much as you hate everyone else' becomes a pragmatic reality. The Israeli is capable of inflicting the ultimate pain on his or her neighbours. In order to understand the tribal concept of self-loving, we must first consider the concept of Chosen-ness.

While the religious (Judaic) understanding of Chosen-ness is interpreted as a moral burden in which Jews are ordered by God to stand as an exemplary model of ethical behaviour, the secular Jewish interpretation has been reduced to a crude, ethno-centric, blood-orientated chauvinism. It encourages those 'lucky' enough to have a Jewish mother to love themselves blindly. In most cases, Israelis interpret their national homecoming as a legitimate dismissal of the elementary rights of the other. In many cases, it leads to animosity and even hatred, whether latent or manifest.

This form of supremacy lies at the heart of the Zionist claim for Palestine, at the expense of its indigenous inhabitants, but it doesn't end there; Jewish Lobbies in the USA and Britain openly advocate for the extension of the 'War Against Terror' against Iran, Islam and beyond. I would never claim that this type of warmongering is inherent to Jews as a people, yet, unfortunately, it is rather symptomatic of Jewish political thinking – left, right and centre. Though Jews are divided between themselves on many issues, they are somehow united in fighting those who they collectively identify as their enemies.

How is it that a people so divided can unite in this way? One explanation has us returning to the idea that Zionism *per se* has little to do with Israel, it is simply an internal Diaspora Jewish discourse. Consequently, the debate between Zionists and so-called 'Jewish anti-Zionists' has zero impact on Israel or the struggle against Israeli policies. It is there to keep the debate 'within the family', while planting more confusion amongst the *Goyim*. It allows the so-called 'progressive' Jewish ethnic campaigner to maintain that 'not all Jews are Zionists'. This dull argument has been good enough to effectively shatter any criticism of Jewish ethnocentric lobbying that may have been voiced in the last four decades.

When it comes to 'action' against the so-called 'enemies of the Jewish people', Zionists and 'Jewish anti-Zionists' act as one people – because they *are* one people. (Whether or not they are, in reality, a single people is irrelevant, as long as they believe themselves to be or act as though they are.) What is it that makes them one people?

There is an old saying: 'Tell me who your friends are, and I'll tell you who you are.' As we saw earlier on, a far more refined reading of Jewish contemporary tribal and identity politics would be: 'Tell me whom you hate, and I'll tell you who you are.' If, for instance, you abhor Norman Finkelstein, Gilad Atzmon, Jeffrey Blankfort, John Mearsheimer and Stephen Walt and so on, you are probably a Jewish ethnic campaigner. If you simply disagree with any of these people, you can actually be anyone.

Chapter 13

The Right to Self-Determination:
A Fake Exercise in Universalism

A few years back, in a little community church in Aspen, Colorado, during the Q&A session that followed a talk I gave, a middle-aged man at the back of the room stood up and introduced himself thus: 'I am a citizen of the world, a cosmopolitan and an atheist. I would like to ask you something, Mr Atzmon'

'Hang on,' I interrupted. 'Please do not be offended by my asking, but are you by any chance a Jew?'

He froze for a second, and couldn't stop from blushing as everyone in the room turned to look at him. I felt a bit guilty about it, because it was not my intention to embarrass the man. It took him a further few seconds to get his act together.

'Yes Gilad, I am a Jew, but how did you know?'

'I obviously didn't know,' I replied. 'I was guessing. You see, whenever I come across people who introduce themselves as "cosmopolitans", "atheists" and "citizens of the world", they somehow always happen to be assimilated "Jews" who identify politically as progressive cosmopolitans. I can only assume that non-Jews find some different methods to deal with discontent related to their identity. If they are born Catholic and decide to move on at a certain stage, they just leave the Church behind. If they do not love their country as much as others do, they probably pack a few things and pick another country to live in. Somehow non-Jews – and this is far from being a scientific observation – do not need to hide behind some vague, universal, abstract banners or righteous value system. But what was your question?'

No question followed. The 'cosmopolitan, atheist and citizen of the world' couldn't remember what his question was. I assume that, following the tradition of post-emancipated Jews, he was there to celebrate his right to 'self-determination' in public. He was going to use the open discussion to tell his Aspen neighbours and friends what a great human being he was. Unlike them, these local patriotic and proud Americans, he was, actually, an advanced human, a man beyond nationhood, a godless, non-patriotic subject, a rational product of the Enlightenment and the true son of Voltaire.

Self-determination is a modern Jewish political and social symptom, even an epidemic. The disappearance of the ghetto and its maternal qualities led to an identity crisis within the largely assimilated Jewish society. Seemingly, all post-emancipated Jewish political, spiritual and social schools of thought, left, right and centre, were inherently concerned with issues to do with the 'right to self-determination'. The Zionists would demand the right to national self-determination at the expense of the Palestinians; the Bund would demand national and cultural self-determination within the Eastern European proletarian discourse; Matzpen, the Israeli ultra-leftists group would demand the right to self-determination for the Israeli Jewish 'nation' in the 'liberated Arab East'; Jewish anti-Zionist would insist upon the right to engage in an esoteric, exclusive, ethnocentric Jewish discourse within the Palestinian solidarity movement.

What does this very right to self-determination stand for? Why is it that modern Jewish secular political thought is grounded on that right? Why is it that some 'progressive' assimilated Jews feel the need to become 'citizens of the world' rather than just ordinary citizens of Britain, France, the USA or Russia?

The Pretence of Authenticity

Although the search for identity and self-determination would seem to suggest a final march toward authentic redemption, the result of identity politics and self-determinative affairs is the precise opposite. As I have said, those who feel compelled to 'self-determine' who they are, are, more than likely, far removed from any authentic self-realisation to start with. Those who identify themselves as 'cosmopolitan', 'progressive', 'secular' or 'humanist' fail to grasp that true human brotherhood needs no introduction or declaration, only genuine love for one another. Genuine and authentic cosmopolitans do not feel the need to declare their abstract commitment to humanism. Real citizens of the world simply live in an open space with no boundaries or borders.

The Right to Self-Determination

The term 'self-determination' was used in the United Nations Charter of 1945, which reads, in part: 'All peoples have the right to freely determine their political status and freely pursue their economic, social and cultural development.' Self-determination has since been defined similarly in various declarations and covenants, and the principle is often regarded as a moral and legal right.

While every human is entitled to celebrate his or her symptoms, the right to self-determination is in fact meaningful only within Western liberal discourse, which accepts such a right and premises it on the notion of enlightened individualism. Such a right is meaningless within a *tribal* discourse. The right to self-determination opposes tribal culture, which gives priority to the survival of the tribe over the celebration of individuality. Jewish politics is captured between these two poles. On the one hand, emancipated Jews insist on celebrating the fruits of enlightenment; they celebrate their right to determine who they are. On the other hand, Jewish politics is tribal, it is intolerant of Jewish dissidence or of any form of self-determination that may oppose what it regards as Jewish political or tribal interests.

The right to self-determination can be celebrated only by the privileged, who are able to mobilise enough political or military power to transform reality. Yet in Western discourse it is only Jews who base their political power on the 'right to be like others'. Zionists insist on being a nation like other nations. The Bund insist on being as proletarian as proletarians anywhere, whereas others prefer to just be themselves – true proletarians do not aspire to the proletariat, and do not need to mimic anyone, they are what they are. Seemingly the entire Jewish political discourse of self-determination is grounded on mimicry. It is thus categorically inauthentic. Consequently, the Jewish notion of self-determination leads its followers into a state of alienation. This may explain the apparent lack of ethical discourse within the realm of Israeli politics and Zionist rhetoric.

In oppressed societies, the right to self-determination is often overshadowed by the impulse to rebel against oppression. For Palestinians in the Occupied Territories and in Gaza, the right to self-determination means less and less. They do not need to self-determine as Palestinians, for they know who they are; if they should happen to forget, the soldiers at the next roadblock are there to remind them. For Palestinians, self-determination is a product of the daily confrontation with the Zionist denial of their most basic elementary rights. It is the right to fight against the occupier, against those who starve and expel them from their land.

As much as the right to self-determination presents itself as an ethical universal political value, in many cases it is used as a divisive and oppressive mechanism resulting in the abuse of others. The Zionist demand for the right to self-determination, for instance, has been openly celebrated at the expense of the Palestinians.

The Bund and Lenin's Criticism

The Bund and the Zionists were the first to eloquently insist upon the Jewish right to self-determination. The General Jewish

Labour Bund of Lithuania, Poland and Russia was, like the Zionist movement, founded in 1897. It maintained that Jews in these countries deserved the right to cultural and national self-determination.

Lenin was probably the first to elaborate on the absurdity of the Jewish demand for self-determination, in his famous attack on the Bund at the Second Congress of the Russian Social-Democratic Labour Party, in 1903. 'March with us,' was his reply to the Bund, rejecting its demand for a special, autonomous ethnic status amongst Russian workers. Lenin had obviously spotted the ethno-centric, divisive and deceitful agenda within Bund philosophy. 'We reject,' said Lenin, 'all obligatory partitions that serve to divide us.' As much as the future founder of the Soviet Union supported 'the right of nations to self-determination'[64], he was clearly dismissive of this right for Jews, which he correctly identified as reactionary – Lenin supported the right of oppressed nations to build their national identities, but resisted any bigoted, narrow, nationalist spirit. His objection to the Bund's demand for cultural self-determination was threefold:

1. Raising the slogan of cultural-national autonomy would lead to the splitting apart of nations, thereby destroying the unity of their proletariat.

2. The intermingling of nations, and their amalgamation, would be a progressive step, while turning away from this goal would be a step backwards. He criticised those who 'cry out to heaven against assimilation'.

3. The 'non-territorial cultural independence' advocated by the Bund and other Jewish parties was not advantageous, practical or practicable.

Using his sharp political common sense, Lenin doubted the

ethical and political grounds of the right to self-determination for Jews, as much as the Bund demanded that Jews should be treated as a national identity like all other nationals. Lenin's answer was simple: 'Sorry, guys, but you aren't. You are not a national minority just because you are unattached to a piece of geography.'

Matzpen and Wolfowitz

'The solution to the national and social problems of this region [The Middle East] ... can come about only through a socialist revolution in this region, which will overthrow all its existing regimes and will replace them by a political union of the region, ruled by the toilers. In this united and liberated Arab East, recognition will be granted to the right of self-determination (including the right to a separate state) of each of the non-Arab nationalities living in the region, including the Israeli-Jewish nation.'[65] –*Twelfth Fundamental Principle, Matzpen (The Socialist Organisation in Israel)*

Lenin's criticism has apparently never been properly internalised by Jewish 'progressive' ideologists and ethnic campaigners.

Reading the declaration of principles formulated by Matzpen, the legendary ultra-leftist Israeli organisation, may leave one perplexed. Already in 1962, the radical Matzpenists had a plan to 'liberate' the Arab world 'through a socialist revolution'. According to Matzpen's principles, all that was needed was to 'overthrow all existing [Arab] regimes' so that 'recognition will be granted to the right of self-determination of each of the non-Arab nationalities living in the region, including the Israeli-Jewish nation'.

It doesn't take a genius to grasp that, at least categorically, Matzpen's principles are no different from Wolfowitz's neocon mantra. Matzpen had a plan to 'overthrow' all Arab regimes in the name of 'socialism'. Wolfowitz would do exactly the same in the name of 'democracy'. Replacing the word 'socialist' with 'democratic' in Matzpen's 'progressive' text gives us a revealing neocon text: 'The solution of the national and social problems of this region, can come about only through a democratic revolution in this region, which will overthrow all its existing regimes and will replace them by a political union of the region ...'

Both the legendarily 'progressive' Matzpen and the 'reactionary' neocons make use of the same abstract concept, with some pretence of universality to justify the Jewish right to self-determination and the destruction of Arab regional power and Islam. Both Matzpen and the neocons profess to know what liberation means for Arabs. For the Matzpenist, to liberate Arabs is to turn them into Bolsheviks; the neocon is actually slightly more modest – all he wants is for Arabs to drink their Coca-Cola in a Westernised democratic society. Both Judeocentric philosophies were doomed to failure, because the notion of self-determination is overwhelmingly *Eurocentric*. Both philosophies are premised on an enlightened notion of individuality and have very little to offer the oppressed except another form of oppression in the name of 'universal' legitimacy. The revolutions taking place in the region currently are far from being socialist or Marxist. Middle East analysts agree that democracy in the Arab World would lead to a far greater representation of Islam within the regional politics, something neocons and Mazpenists would not welcome.

Matzpen has never had any political power or significance, and has never been in any proximity to Arab masses. Consequently, Matzpen could never affect the lives of Arabs; nor could it destroy their regimes. However, Matzpen is seen by Jewish leftists around the world as a significant 'intellectual' chapter in Jewish progressive thought. It is also regarded as a singular and significant moment of Israeli ethical awakening. It is acutely embarrassing, therefore, to discover that this most enlightened and refined moment of Jewish Marxism, or Israeli-leftist moral awakening, has produced a political insight that is no different, categorically, to George Bush's attempt to 'liberate' the Iraqi people. It should be clear beyond doubt that Jewish ultra-leftism (à la Matzpen) and Zionist-influenced Anglo–American 'moral interventionism' (à la neoconservatism) are only two sides of the same *shekel*. They are theoretically, ideologically and pragmatically very close as political thought – Judeo-centric to the bone yet supposedly premised on universalism with the aim of 'liberation' and 'freedom'. At the end of the day, what we see here is a Judeo-centric political exercise, namely self-determination, which comes at the expense of others.

Chapter 14

Milton Friedman Revisited

During the 1960s-80s Milton Friedman was regarded by many academics, politicians and world leaders as the most important post-World War II economist. Friedman was Chief Economic Advisor to Ronald Reagan, Margaret Thatcher and Menachem Begin. He also went on the record advising the Chilean military dictator Augusto Pinochet.

It is far from surprising that more and more commentators have realised in recent years that it was Friedman's ideology and advocacy of free enterprise, zero governmental intervention, avoidance of regulation and privatisation that has led to the current financial turmoil. It was Milton Friedman's philosophy that also contributed to the transformation of the West into a service economy.

But Friedman wasn't just an economist: he was also a devout Zionist and a very proud Jew. Friedman was interested in the role of the Jews in world finance and politics. He also attempted to analyse and understand the attitude of Jews towards wealth. In 1972 Friedman spoke to the Mont Pelerin Society about 'Capitalism and the Jews'[66]. In 1978 he repeated the same talk, addressing Jewish students at Chicago University's Hillel institute.[67]

The Jewish Paradox

Friedman was, no doubt, a sharp intellect and could offer succinct criticism. Yet he was not exactly 'a cosmopolitan', since he was deeply involved in Jewish concerns and Zionist affairs, and open and transparent about being so.

In the talks he gave in 1972 and 1978, Friedman examined a

unique Jewish paradox: 'Here are two propositions,' he said. 'Each of them is validated by evidence yet they are both incompatible one with the other.'

The first proposition is that 'there are few peoples, if any, in the world who owe so great a debt to free enterprise and competitive capitalism as the Jews.'

The second proposition is that 'there are few peoples, or any, in the world who have done so much to undermine the intellectual foundation of capitalism as the Jews.'

How do we reconcile these two contradictory propositions?

Friedman, the free enterprise advocate, was convinced that monopoly and government intervention were bad news in general; but, more crucially for him, they were also very bad for the Jews.

'Wherever there is a monopoly, whether it be private or governmental, there is room for the application of arbitrary criteria in the selection of the beneficiaries of the monopoly – whether these criteria be color of skin, religion, national origin or what not. Where there is free competition, only performance counts.'

Friedman clearly prefers competition. According to him, 'the market is colour-blind. No one who goes to the market to buy bread knows or cares whether the wheat was grown by a Jew, Catholic, Protestant, Muslim, or atheist, by whites or blacks.'

Friedman elaborates further: 'Any miller who wishes to express his personal prejudices by buying only from preferred groups is at a competitive disadvantage, since he is keeping himself from buying from the cheapest source. He can express his prejudice, but he will have to do so at his own expense, accepting a lower monetary income than he could otherwise earn.'

'Jews,' Friedman continues, 'have flourished most in those countries in which competitive capitalism had the greatest scope: Holland in the sixteenth and seventeenth centuries, and Britain and the U.S. in the nineteenth and twentieth centuries, Germany in the late nineteenth and early twentieth century.'

According to Friedman, it is also no accident that Jews suffered the most in Nazi Germany and Soviet Russia, for these countries defied free market ideology.

One may suggest at this point that, though it is undoubtedly true that Jews suffered in Soviet Russia and in Nazi Germany, and though it is also true that these countries defied free market ideology, Friedman fails to establish a causal or even rational relationship between the opposition to the free market, and anti-Jewish policies.

However, the message Friedman conveys is clear – Jews do benefit from hard capitalism and competitive markets.

Yet Friedman is also genuinely intrigued by Jewish intellectuals' affinity with anti-capitalism: 'Jews have been a stronghold of anti-capitalist sentiment. From Karl Marx through Leon Trotsky to Herbert Marcuse, a sizable fraction of the revolutionary anti-capitalist literature has been authored by Jews.'

Ideology vs. Opportunism

How could that be, Friedman wonders? Why is it that, despite the historical record of the benefits of competitive capitalism to the Jews, despite the intellectual explanation of this phenomenon that is implicit or explicit in much liberal literature from at least Adam Smith onwards, the Jews have been disproportionately anti-capitalist?

Friedman considers some answers: 'Rather often we hear from Jews on the left that their affinity to humanitarian issues is driven by their "Jewish humanist heritage"'. More than once I myself have commented that this is an utter lie. There is no such a Jewish heritage. Driven by tribal precepts, both Judaism and 'Jewish ideology' are devoid of universal ethics. If there are some remote patches of humanism in Jewish culture, these are certainly far from being universal.

Friedman, however, offered a further take on the subject. In direct reference to Lawrence Fuchs, who argues that the anti-capitalism of the Jews is a 'direct reflection of values derived from the Jewish religion and culture,' Friedman wonders, if Jewish culture is, indeed, inherently anti-capitalist (as Fuchs suggests), how is it then that Jews failed to successfully combat Capitalism and free markets throughout their history? Friedman analyses that whilst 'Jewish religion and culture date back over two millennia, the Jewish opposition to capitalism and attachment to socialism, is at the most, less than two centuries old.'

Being a sharp intellect, Friedman managed to dismantle Fuchs's argument. He managed to counter the argument that Jewish culture is inherently socialist or humanist: if Judaism is, indeed, inherently and innately bound to such ethics, how is it that this humanism failed to become dominant throughout Jewish history?

Friedman also reflects, in a surprisingly respectful manner, on the writing of alleged anti-Semite Werner Sombart's *The Jews and Modern Capitalism*. Sombart identifies Jewish ideology at the heart of capitalism. 'Throughout the centuries, the Jews championed the cause of individual liberty in economic activity, against the dominating view of the time. The individual was not to be hampered by regulations of any sort. I think that the Jewish religion has the same leading ideas as capitalism . . .' [68]

Though Jewish intellectuals at the time were largely unhappy with Sombart's book, Milton Friedman is brave enough to admit that there is nothing in the book itself to justify any charge of anti-Semitism (though, he argues, there certainly is in Sombart's later work). Friedman, a proud capitalist, tends actually to interpret Sombart's book as 'philo-Semitic'.

'If, like me', says Friedman, 'you regard competitive capitalism as the economic system that is most favorable to individual freedom, to creative accomplishments in technology and the arts, and to the widest possible opportunities for the ordinary man, then you will regard Sombart's assignment to the

Jews of a key role in the development of capitalism as high praise. You will, as I do, regard his book as philo-Semitic.'

Milton Friedman may even agree with early Marx, that Capitalism is Jewish 'by nature'. Yet while Marx believed that in order for the world to liberate itself from Capitalism it had better emancipate itself from the Jews[69], for Friedman capitalism is of profound value and to be respected, thus Jews should be praised for their inherent bond with this philosophy and its diverse ramifications. As far as Friedman is concerned, for Capitalism to prevail, Jews should continue to do what they are good at, and that is to trade freely in an open and competitive market.

Friedman seems to dismiss the presumed 'intellectual honesty' behind Jewish affiliation with the left and anti-capitalism. He tends to argue that the Jewish intellectual inclination towards the left is a direct outcome of certain political and historical circumstances, rather than ethical or ideological choice. He explains that, in his view, Jewish affiliation with the left is the product of a particular occurrence in Europe in the nineteenth century.

'Beginning with the era of the French revolution, the European political spectrum became divided into a "Left" and a "Right" along an axis that involved the issue of secularism. The Right (conservative, monarchical, "clerical") maintained that there must be a place for the church in the public order; the left (democratic, liberal, radical) held that there can be no church at all . . .'

It was only natural, then, for the Jews to join the left – in fact Jews could *only* join the left.

'The axis separating left from right also formed a natural boundary for the pale of Jewish political participation. It was the left, with its new secular concept of citizenship, that had accomplished the Emancipation, and it was only the left that could see a place for the Jews in public life.'

Such a reasoning, then, views Jewish affiliation with the left as a politically opportunistic move instead of a form of 'moral awakening'.

This reading of the 'Jewish left' reaffirms my own critical assessment. It also explains why some Jews join the left – they support cosmopolitanism, solidarity, an international working class; and yet they themselves often seem to prefer to operate within 'Jews only' racially-orientated cells such as the Bund, Jewish Socialists or even Jews for Boycott of Israeli Goods. Friedman's reasoning might also explain why so many Jews who had their roots in the so-called 'left', ended up preaching moral interventionism and neo-conservatism.

Friedman also argues that Jewish affiliation with the left might be better understood as an attempt to disown some anti-Semitic stereotypes of the Jew as being 'a merchant or moneylender who put commercial interests ahead of human values.'

According to Friedman, the Jewish anti-capitalist is there to prove that, far from being money-grabbing, selfish and heartless, Jews are really public-spirited, generous, and concerned with ideals rather than material goods. 'How better to do so than to attack the market, with its reliance on monetary values and impersonal transactions, and to glorify the political process, to take as an ideal a state run by well-meaning people for the benefit of their fellow men?'

And yet, in Friedman's logic then, it is not a 'moral awakening' that moves the Jew to the left; it is neither humanism, nor solidarity and nor is it kindness, but, instead, it seems to be a desperate attempt to replace or amend the Jewish image.

Surprisingly enough, I find myself in total agreement with Friedman, though I would phrase it differently. I do differentiate between 'the leftist who happens to be Jewish' – an innocent category[70] inspired by humanism, and 'the Jewish leftist'[71], which seems to me to be a contradiction in terms, for the left aims to universally transcend itself beyond ethnicity, religion or race.

Clearly 'Jewish left' is there to maintain a Jewish tribal ethno-centric identity at the heart of working class philosophy.

Seemingly then, Friedman managed to resolve the paradox between his two initial propositions (Jews being the benefactors of capitalism vs. Jews being profoundly anti-capitalist) by offering an historical and political explanation: Jews or Jewish intellectuals are not really against capitalism, it was just the 'special circumstances of the nineteenth century that drove Jews to the left, and the subconscious attempts by Jews to demonstrate to themselves and the world the fallacy of the anti-Semitic stereotype'. It was neither ideology nor ethics.

This interpretation explains why leftist Zionism was doomed to disappear. During his talks, Friedman reviewed the right/left political division in Israel. He noticed that two opposing traditions were at work in the Jewish State: an ancient one, going back nearly two thousand years, of finding ways around govern-mental restrictions, and a modern one, going back a century, of belief in 'democratic socialism' and 'central planning'. Friedman was clever enough to gather already in 1972 that it is the 'Jewish tradition', rather than socialism, that would prevail. Friedman noticed already in the 1970s that Israel was capitalist to the bone. He predicted that the short phase of Zionist 'pseudo-socialism' was foreign to Jewish culture.

Yet it isn't just the Israeli left that was doomed to die. Friedman's reading of Jewish culture also explains why the Bund died – it didn't really spread to the West – which also explains why Mazpen and other Jewish anti-Zionist revolutionary groups have never attracted the Jewish masses.

Self-Fulfilling Prophecy

Friedman is not free of fault. In spite of his succinct reading of the Jewish left/right divide, there are a few crucial points that have to be made about Friedman's take on Jewish culture, and his examination of capitalism.

Friedman argues that the free market and competition is good for the Jews. Yet he is also adamant that Government intervention is a disaster that leads to anti-Semitism and other forms of institutional bigotry. If Friedman's model is valid, then Jews in the West had better brace themselves, for Western Governments are currently desperately intervening in the markets, in an attempt to slow down the inevitable collapse of what is left of our economy and relative wealth.

If Friedman's model is correct, and intervention is indeed bad for the Jews, then anti-Jewish bigotry could be imminent, especially considering the gigantic bailout intervention schemes put up by states in an attempt to save what remains of the Western economy.

But it goes further – it is also very clear that the bailout schemes are there to amend a colossal disaster caused largely by the endorsement of Friedman's own ideology. We are all paying a very heavy price for free enterprise, zero (governmental) intervention, lack of regulation, hard capitalism – in general, the ideologies Friedman was so enthusiastic about.

There is something Friedman didn't tell his listeners in the 1970s: he himself probably did not realise the full meaning of his economic model. He did not realise that the adoption of his philosophy by Ronald Reagan and Margaret Thatcher would eventually bring the West to its knees. He did not realise that it was his own advocacy of hard capitalism that would lead Western continents to poverty and deprivation. He perhaps did not realise, back in the 1970s, that it was his model that would eventually eliminate productivity, and every positive aspect of the welfare state. Milton Friedman did not realise, at that time, that a service economy that had suited some ethnic minorities for two millennia wouldn't necessarily be successful once adopted into a macro model. As Friedman had gathered, throughout their history Jews and other ethnic minorities were very effective operating a service economy within competitive and productive markets. However, Jews and other ethnic or religious minorities did well because others were there to work around them. The transformation of the West into a service economy driven by relentless greed, a process that followed Friedman's economic precepts, is now proving to be a disaster. It means poverty and global depression. It is translated into alienation from labour and productivity.

Friedman may have been correct when he predicted that governmental intervention may lead to anti-Semitism, yet he probably failed to realise that it was largely his own intellectual heritage that would be responsible for the current financial disaster. It is, in fact, his own economic model and prophecy that could introduce Jews to far more suffering.

Chapter 15

Swindler's List

The following verse, from *Deuteronomy* 6:10-12, is a part of an oration made by Moses to his people while on their way to the 'Promised Land':

'Then when the Lord your God brings you to the land he promised your ancestors Abraham, Isaac, and Jacob to give you – a land with large, fine cities you did not build, houses filled with choice things you did not accumulate, hewn out cisterns you did not dig, and vineyards and olive groves you did not plant – and you eat your fill, be careful not to forget the Lord who brought you out of Egypt, that place of slavery.'

The Judaic God, as portrayed by Moses in the above passage, is an evil deity, who leads his people to plunder, robbery and theft. Yet there are many ways to deal with this negative image of the Almighty. At the literary level, one can argue that the given verses are no more than just three isolated lines in a lengthy text that is well-meaning and offers some fundamental universal thoughts. At the contextual level, it may be suggested that it wasn't actually God speaking to the Chosen People, but Moses himself, who failed to deliver the true divine message – in other words, Moses may have got it wrong, or even made it up. There are many other ways to save the Judaic God and Judaism from being the *logos* behind contemporary Israeli plunder, but it is not so easy to save the Israelis from being presented as robbers and pillagers.

Moses, his contemporaries and their current followers were and are excited about the possibilities that awaited them in the Land of Milk and Honey. Israel, the Jewish State, has been following Moses' call. The ethnic cleansing of the Palestinian people in 1948, and the constant and total abuse of the Palestinian people since then, makes *Deuteronomy* 6:10–12 look like a prophecy fulfilled.

For more than sixty years, the Biblical call for theft has been put into legal *praxis*. The Israeli looting of Palestinian cities, homes, fields and wells has found its way into Israel's legal system: by 1950-51, Israeli legislators had already approved the 'Absentee Property Law', a racially-orientated law preventing Palestinians from returning to their lands, cities and villages, and allowing the new Israelites to live in houses and cities they 'did not build'.

The never-ending theft of Palestine in the name of the Jewish people is part of a spiritual, ideological, cultural and practical continuum between the Bible, Zionist ideology and the State of Israel (along with its overseas supporters). Israel and Zionism, both successful political systems, have instituted the plunder promised by the Hebrew God in the Judaic holy scriptures.

But this continuum goes further than just theft – in reviewing the following Biblical passages, recall the devastating images of Gazans being bombed in a UN shelter at the time of the IDF's Operation Cast Lead (Dec-Jan 2008-2009):

'You will chase your enemies, and they shall fall by the sword before you. Five of you shall chase a hundred, and a hundred of you shall put ten thousand to flight; your enemies shall fall by the sword before you.' *Leviticus, 26:7–8*

'When the Lord your God brings you into the land you are entering to possess and drives out before you many nations … you must destroy them totally. Make no treaty with them, and show them no mercy.' *Deuteronomy 7:1–2*

'Do not leave alive anything that breathes. Completely destroy

them ... as the Lord your God has commanded you ...'
Deuteronomy 20:16

There is no doubt amongst Biblical scholars that the Hebrew Bible contains some highly-charged, unethical suggestions, some of which are no less than calls for genocide. The Catholic theologian Raymund Schwager found 600 passages of explicit violence in the Old Testament, along with 1000 descriptive verses of God's own violent punishments and 100 passages where God expressly commands others to kill. Violence is one of the most frequently mentioned activities in the Hebrew Bible.

Secular Israelis do not follow Judaic law, yet they somehow collectively interpret their Jewish identity as a Biblical mission, which perhaps sheds some light on the IDF massacres in Gaza and Lebanon in the last few years. The IDF used lethal methods, such as cluster bombs and white phosphorus, against civilians as though its main objective was to 'destroy' while showing 'no mercy' whatsoever. It seems as though the Israeli military, in erasing northern Gaza in January 2009, were following *Deuteronomy* 20:16 – they did indeed 'not leave alive anything that breathe[d]'. Yet *why* should a secular commander follow *Deuteronomy* verses or any other Biblical text?

Though most Jews do not follow the Bible, and many are even ignorant of its content, the lethal spirit of the scriptures has infused the essence of modern Jewish political discourse. Those who disagree with such a generalisation may invoke the Bund and its 'progressive', secular, 'ethical' and cosmopolitan heritage, but a quick glance at the Bund's heritage reveals that it is not fundamentally different from Zionism. Bundists believe that instead of robbing Palestinians, Jews should all unite and appropriate from the wealthy classes, the strong, in the name of working-class revolution. Here is the Bund's call for action, taken from its anthem, 'The Vow':

We swear our stalwart hate persists,
Of those who rob and kill the poor:
The Tsar, the masters, capitalists.
Our vengeance will be swift and sure.
So swear together to live or die!

On the face of it, confiscating the homes and wealth of the rich is regarded as an ethical act, at least within Bundist discourse – possessing more is a crime.

As a young man, I myself took part in some Jewish righteous parades, ready to grab my sword and join the hunt for a Tsar, a capitalist or any other enemy who might cross my way. But then the inevitable happened: I grew up. I realised that such vengeance toward an entire class of wealthy *goyim* is no more than an extension of God's exhortations via Moses in *Deuteronomy*.

As we can see, robbery and hatred is imbued in Jewish modern political ideology on both the left and the right. One must agree that, at least from an ethical point of view, theft cannot be the way forward, whether from Palestinians, Iraqis or even the Tsar himself[72]. Theft involves a categorical dismissal of the other, even when it is based on an inherent self-righteousness.

As far as unethical practice is concerned, the difference between Judaism and contemporary Jewish nationalism can be illustrated as follows: while the Judaic Biblical context is filled with references to violent deeds, usually committed in the name of God, within the modern Jewish national and political context Jews kill and rob in their own name, in the name of self-determination, 'working class politics', 'Jewish suffering' and national aspirations. Here is the ultimate success of the Jewish national revolution: it taught the Jews to believe in themselves. 'The Israeli' robs in the name of 'home-coming', the progressive Jew in the name of 'Marx', and the moral interventionist murders in the name of 'democracy'.

Historicity & Factuality vs. Fantasy & Phantasm

Chapter 16

Trauma Queen

A few years back, an American Jewish feminist academic sent me a request for an interview. I love interviews – they save me from having to go to shrinks. The professor presented herself as a 'gender scholar', another postmodernist discipline that fails to inspire my intellect. However, I was curious to see what a person who happens to be academically qualified in being a woman might come up with.

A few days later, a questionnaire appeared in my email inbox. The professor had loaded me with queries regarding my military experience and my 'post-traumatic' state. Evidently she was convinced that I was a case of Post-Traumatic Stress Disorder (Post-TSD). I admit this took me by surprise – I have never spoken to anyone about my 'post-traumatic' symptoms – for the very good reason that, until that point in time, I had never been aware of myself as suffering any traumatic disorders whatsoever.

I was intrigued by her approach. Apparently she was comparing military veterans' Post-TSD cases with traumatised female rape victims. At the same time, I wondered how she had managed to identify me as a suitable candidate for her research. I then realised that her perception of me as traumatised was probably the outcome of her encounter with my first novel, *A Guide to the Perplexed*.

In that book, I describe the protagonist Günter Wunker's wartime experience. In the midst of battle, Günter is shattered by fear, and finds a shelter behind a rock. Eventually he shoots his own leg in a chaotic attack. I remember being thrilled when writing those lines – it all sounded close to home. Throughout my life I have watched many war films and read many war books. I had been close enough to a battlefield myself, and had thirstily interviewed many soldiers, but I have never been in battle. When my time came to serve my country and offer my life on the Jewish altar, I caved in; I became more and more attached to my different organs, especially to the ones that stick out.

Obviously, then, Günter's battlefield experience was *fictional*. It had nothing to do with my own personal experience of the military. I *invented* it all. This is what fiction writers do. Yet that one specific scene must have seemed authentic to this American professor. She seemed to believe that Günter was a literary vehicle for my own story.

In confronting the question of my supposed military-induced trauma, it became clear to me that a 'trauma' and a *traumatic biographic event* are two distinct categories that are not necessarily associated. I found myself recollecting my army experience, along with the years that followed it, and found that there *was* one fright, which had taken me ages to overcome.

Until my early thirties, bombs would occasionally fall overhead in my dreams. While asleep I would run for my life across an endless, open field. I could clearly envisage Syrian Mig fighter jets, sometimes flying so low that the pilots' faces were visible. The bombs were dropped in vast quantities. In my dreams I zigzagged on the ground, craning my head upward to watch for deadly iron. I would sprint, fall down, crawl, stand up, run, drop down, fall and run again. My nights saw me speeding through burning fields dodging shrapnel until, eventually, one of the bombs would plunge onto my head, and I would awaken from the blaze in one piece though covered in cold sweat. The nightmares faded soon after I left Israel; I didn't experience another one for a very long time.

However, it is important to note that, as far as my biography is concerned, I have never *been* subject to an air raid. Not one single enemy plane has ever chased me or bombarded me. My bomb dreams were not a reaction to any real, objective event, quite the opposite, in fact: they were probably a reaction to a *non-event*.

Unless these dreams can be interpreted as resulting from fear of impotence or some other anxiety over libidinal regression, I can guess where and how their seeds were planted. Once, during the 1982 war in Lebanon, as part of a convoy to the *Chouf* Mountains, we were ordered to jump out of the safari trucks in what was assumed to be an air raid alert. As a bunch of clueless soldiers, we knew very little about air raids; we copied the combatants around us and dug ourselves into an open field, looking for shelter and praying to God. The Syrian planes never made it to our convoy, in the end, but the unresolved terror stayed in my mind for a long time. It formulated into an imaginary discourse saturated with symbolism, traumatic implications and a sweaty outcome.

This fright perhaps found its way into my fiction. When conveying Günter's horror I relived this fear that was self-constructed, a product of my own psyche. I merely amplified the scene.

The American scholar who mistakenly interpreted Günter's horror as an expression of a biographical, personal trauma opened my eyes to the nature of trauma itself. I became somehow suspicious of so-called 'traumatised people', and even more suspicious of 'traumatised nations'. I realised that being in a state of a trauma doesn't necessarily imply a 'real' catalyst of objective biographical experience. Biography is a form of imposition, the projection of a post-dated set of ideas, feeling and thoughts. It conveys the past we *want* to posses rather than the past we lived through. (My second novel, *My One and Only Love*, was, in fact, an attempted critique of the notion of personal biography and personal narrative. The plot is structured according to three parallel narratives, all referring to the same historical events but conveying completely different biographical accounts.)

Unlike many Post-TSD experts, I tend to dismiss the magical bond between trauma and biography. Trauma doesn't necessarily imply a verifiable traumatic event. The fact that a few scholars base their analysis of Israeli identity on some sort of collective Jewish trauma doesn't mean that Jews are indeed traumatised by their past. It is far more likely that they are traumatised by their imaginary future.

Pre-Traumatic Gas Syndrome

One of the most terrifying moments in Steven Spielberg's *Schindler's List* is, doubtless, the gas chamber sequence. Earlier in the film, rumours had been circulating to the effect that Jews are being gassed to death. Now, anxious women are sent naked to the showers in Auschwitz. We follow their death march; we are familiar with the Holocaust's symbolic order, we all know what 'showers' stand for. We anticipate a homicidal Nazi crime. A moment later we are relieved, as they are, when instead of Zyklon B, water pours down onto their heads. The strength of the cinematic moment is down to the gulf between the pre-traumatic imaginary narrative and the reality onscreen. In other words, the trauma predates the traumatic event; the trauma itself shapes the reality.

I was raised amongst people my age who insisted upon being traumatised: the 'third generation' they call themselves. People like myself, who were born in the 1960s or later, way after the liberation of Auschwitz. People who claim to have been afflicted by events that neither they nor their parents had experienced. Isn't that strange? As I revealed here, I myself was tormented by an air raid that never occurred. The difference is that I stopped short of blaming the Syrian air force for planting these air raid images in my dreams.

Pre-Traumatic Stress Syndrome (Pre-TSS) is a fundamental tenet of Jewish and Israeli culture. Young Israelis are transported to Auschwitz by different Zionist organisations for the purpose of maturing into traumatised Jewish adults. Those who maintain these 'educational' trips know that trauma is a powerful fuel with which to maintain the Zionist narrative. Unfortunately, the Israeli youngsters implement the wrong lesson once they return and join the IDF. Rather than developing some empathetic feelings towards victims of oppression, i.e. the Palestinians, the tormented Isreali youth actually seem to mimic SS brutality. 'Never Again' they say, and then spread misery around them.

Back in 2006 Israeli Journalist Yair Sheleg managed to sketch an exemplary case of Pre-Traumatic Stress Syndrome.

'It is hard to believe, but only 60 years after the Holocaust the Jewish people are once again in danger of being destroyed – at least in their own state, where 40 percent of the world's Jews are concentrated. Evidence of the severity of the danger can be found not only in the explicit threats by Iran's president, which are backed up by an arms program that would provide the means to carry them out. It can also be found in recent articles in the European press that discuss the possibility of Israel's 'disappearance' as a reasonable 'working assumption.' Additional evidence regarding the threat level exists in the fact that not only is Israel the only country in the world that is threatened with destruction, it is also the only state whose right to exist is the focus of international polls, with many respondents answering negatively. That is an honour that not even Iran, North Korea and apartheid-era South Africa were ever granted.'[73]

Though it may be that a growing number of people want to see an end to Israel, no one in political or media circles is calling for the destruction of the Jews or the Israeli people. The well-established Judeo-centric tendency to interpret almost any political and ideological criticism as a declaration of impending Judeocide is a severe form of collective Pre-TSS.

Is Pre-TSS just another name for paranoia? I would argue no. People suffering from paranoia inspire our sympathy or pity. Paranoiacs are victims of their own symptoms. Sufferers of Pre-TSS, on the other hand, actually celebrate their symptoms at others' expense. With paranoia we can determine clearly that the sufferer is trapped in a delusional world. However, those with Pre-TSS are supposedly healthy, they are on constant alert and seem to be very focused. Often we end up believing the Pre-TSS sufferer's claims of being victimised by an imagined future crime, thus participating in someone else's fantasy of destruction. In the case of Pre-TSS, we are the addressees as long as we remain silent. Once we raise our voices to point out that the imaginary future crime is yet to happen and actually may never happen, we immediately become part of the crime ourselves.

The general mood in Israel is expressed eloquently by the likes of Sheleg, and reflected in the catastrophic scenarios put forward by such parties as the American Jewish Committee, about Iran's nuclear ambitions. Israel and its lobbies have been publicly fixated on the nuclear *Shoah* to come. This pathological obsession is strange considering the fact that Hezbollah managed to defeat the mighty IDF in Lebanon (2006) with only light weaponry and smart tactics. It also managed to panic Israeli society with nothing more than short-range Katyusha rockets. In fact, Israel's enemies do not need to nuke the country – all they need do is send a message to the Jews of the world that Israel is anything but a shelter. In fact, this is what Arab and Islamic resistance is all about: a metaphysical message rather than a call for a Judeocide.

Interestingly enough, the fear of destruction set by the condition of the Pre-TSS is just another escape route from reality. Rather than facing any imminent danger posed by Hezbollah, Hamas and Islamic resistance, Israel prefers to amplify a phantasmic trauma. The Israelis have failed to read the writing on the wall. Rather than looking in the mirror and spotting their faults (which have matured into moral bankruptcy), they prefer to submit to the fantasy of nuclear Judeocide. Rather than thinking in ethical terms, they surrender to the shallowest materialist discourse solely centred on an illusionary theme, namely, the 'destruction of the I'.

Projection and Pre-TSS

Following the 2nd Lebanon war, a commander of an IDF rocket unit in Lebanon told *Ha'aretz* newspaper, 'What we did was insane and monstrous, we covered entire towns in cluster bombs ... the IDF fired around 1,800 cluster bombs, containing over 1.2 million cluster bomblets.'[74]

As no-one is actually voicing a call to throw the Israelis into the sea or to nuke them, Israel's inclination to blame Muslims and Arabs for holding such murderous tendencies themselves must then be understood in terms of *projection*. The people who rained Lebanon in 2006 with more than a million cluster bombs and showered Gaza with white phosphorus (2008-9) are projecting their homicidal zeal onto their victims, and even onto their future victims. This dynamic can be easily explained. The more pain we inflict on others the more we become familiar with evil, aggression and brutality. The more cruel we are towards others, the more horrified we are by the possibility that the subjects of our brutality may also be as nasty as we are. Freud calls it projection. Otto Weininger refined it, 'we hate in others, that which we don't like in ourselves'. The dynamic of projection is amplified once the subject of our terror is hopeless and defenceless.

Israeli treatment of the Palestinians is a devastating example of the above. The more hopeless and defenseless the Palestinians are, the more vicious the Israeli becomes. And yet, the more vicious the Israeli is, the more he or she is horrified by 'terror'. In reality, the Israelis are actually horrified by their own cruelty. It is the terror within that horrifies the most. The recent cold-blooded murder of nine peace activists, on the high seas, by Israeli Navy Seal commandos[75] was a shocking exposure of that lethal dynamic. This astonishing attack was fuelled by an imaginary terror threat (pre-TSS). The viciousness of the Israeli commando was amplified by the innocent transparency of the Gaza fleet.

One may wonder whether there is an escape route out of this vicious circle? Is there any means to dismantle the phantasmic fear of the other being as brutal as I happen to be? I guess that 'turn the other cheek' is a valid way to defy the Old Testament's 'eye for an eye'. Turning the other cheek is commonly realised as a means to counter an aggressor. However, it maybe the only possible measure to dismantle the 'terror within', that aggression that brews inside us as we become vindictive. It can also be very effective in defusing our anger at an imaginary threat. We replace it with acceptance, we disarm ourselves. We give peace a chance.

Comic Relief

> Jewish Telegram: 'Begin Worrying, Details to Follow.' - *Old Joke*

The joke above – older than Israel, and probably as old as the telegraph itself – refers to the dialectic of fear that dominates the Jewish political and ideological mindset. Fear has been exploited politically by Jewish leaders since the early days of emancipation. However, it is possible that during the process of Jewish secular-isation and emancipation initiated by the Enlightenment and the French Revolution, fear of imaginary doom replaced the fear of Almighty God, the God of Sodom and Gomorrah who kills without mercy. If this is indeed the case, 'fear' might be recog-nised as one of the many modern Jewish Gods, and Pre-TSS as modern Jewish practice.

Chapter 17

The Wandering Who?

Tel Aviv University historian Professor Shlomo Sand opens his remarkable study of Jewish nationalism, *The Invention of the Jewish People*, by quoting Karl Deutsch: 'A nation … is a group of persons united by a common error about their ancestry and a common dislike of their neighbours.'[76]

As simple or even as simplistic as it may seem, this quote eloquently summarises modern Jewish nationalism and especially the concept of Jewish identity. It points the finger at the collective mistake Jews tend to make whenever referring to their illusory 'collective past' or 'collective origin'.

In his book, Sand posits a serious doubt that the Jewish people ever existed as a nation or race, ever shared a common origin. Instead, they are a colourful mix of groups that, at various stages throughout history, adopted the Jewish religion. So when were the Jewish people 'invented'? Sand's answer: 'At a certain stage in the 19th century, intellectuals of Jewish origin in Germany, influenced by the folk character of German nationalism, took upon themselves the task of inventing a people 'retrospectively,' out of a thirst to create a modern Jewish people.'[77]

Accordingly, the 'Jewish people' is a made-up notion, consisting of an imaginary past with very little to back it up forensically, historically or textually. Furthermore, Sand, who elaborated on early sources from antiquity, comes to the conclusion that Jewish exile is also a myth, and that the present-day Palestinians are far more likely to be the descendants of the ancient Semitic people in Judea/Canaan than the current, predominantly Khazarian-origin, Ashkenazi crowd, which he admits he belongs to himself.

Hitler Won After All

Supposedly secular, cosmopolitan Jews often retort, when asked what it is that makes them Jewish, that 'Hitler made me a Jew.' Though 'cosmopolitans' tend to dismiss other people's national inclinations, Jewish cosmopolitans, for some reason, insist on maintaining their own right to 'self-determination'. It is not really they themselves who stand at the core of this unique demand for national orientation, but the Devil, the master-monster anti-Semite, Adolf Hitler. Apparently, cosmopolitan Jews can celebrate their nationalist entitlement as long as Hitler is there to be blamed. Hitler won, then, after all.

Shlomo Sand illuminates this paradox. Insightfully, he suggests that 'there were times in Europe when anyone who argued that all Jews belong to a nation of alien origin would have been classified at once as an anti-Semite. Nowadays, anyone who dares to suggest that the people known in the world as Jews (as distinct from today's Israelis) have never been, and are still not, a people or a nation is immediately denounced as a Jew hater.'[78] In Israel, Jews celebrate their unique differentiation from other peoples. In fact, even the Jewish anti-Zionists enhance their distinct characteristics in comparison to other peace activists.

Nationalism and Jewish Nationalism

Louis-Ferdinand Céline wrote that during the Middle Ages, between the major wars, knights would charge a very high price for their readiness to die in the name of their kingdoms; in the twentieth century, however, youngsters rushed to die *en masse* without demanding a thing in return. Understanding this shift in mass consciousness requires an eloquent, methodical model that allows us to understand what nationalism *is*.

Like Karl Deutsch, Sand regards nationality as a phantasmal narrative. Anthropological and historical studies of the origins of different so-called 'peoples' and 'nations' lead, embarrassingly, to the crumbling of every ethnicity and ethnic identity. It is therefore rather interesting to discover that many Jews tend to take their own ethnic myth very seriously. I can think of two possible explanations for this insistence. One was offered by Israeli academic Benjamin Beit-Hallahmi years ago. Zionism, he said, was there to transform the Bible from a spiritual text into a 'land registry'. The second explanation is psychoanalytical: it is actually the lack of factuality or coherent historical narrative that leads to the emergence of such a phantasmic tale, strong will and a pragmatic agenda to follow.

The lack of ethnic origin doesn't stop people from feeling ethnic or national belonging. The fact that Jews are far from being what one can label a 'people', and that the Bible has very little historical truth in it, doesn't really stop generations of Israelis and/or Jews from identifying themselves as the sons and daughters of King David or Samson.

In the 1970s, Shlomo Artzi, then a young Israeli singer destined to become Israel's all-time greatest rock star, released 'Pitom Kam Adam' ('Suddenly a Man Wakes Up'), a song that became a smash hit in a matter of hours. Here is a translation of the first few lines:

Suddenly a man wakes up in the morning/
He feels he is a nation, and begins to walk/
And to everyone he meets along the way/
He calls out, 'Shalom.'

To a certain extent, in his lyrics, Artzi innocently expresses the suddenness of the transformation of the Jews into 'a people'. However, at the same time, Artzi contributes to the illusory national myth of the peace-seeking nation. The Israeli singer should have known by then that Jewish nationalism was a violent, expansionist act at the expense of the indigenous Palestinian people. It didn't really say *shalom* to anyone except superpowers.

There Is No Jewish History

It is an established fact that virtually no Jewish history texts were written between the first and early-nineteenth centuries. That Judaism is based on a religious historical myth may have something to do with this. An adequate scrutiny of the Jewish past was never a primary concern in the rabbinical tradition – the absence of any need for such a methodical effort probably accounts for this. For Jews during ancient times and the Middle Ages, there was enough in the Bible to answer most relevant questions having to do with day-to-day life, Jewish meaning and fate. As Sand puts it: 'A chronological sequence of events was alien to the (Jewish) exilic time – a condition of constant alertness, attuned to the longed-for moment when the Messiah would appear.'[79] This apparent lack of Jewish interest in history, historicity and chronology is crucial for the understanding of Jewish political identity.

In light of German secularisation, urbanisation and emancipation, and given the decreasing authority of rabbinical leaders, the need for an alternative cause emerged amongst awakening Jewish intellectuals: emancipated Jews wondered who they were and where they came from. They also began to speculate on the role of Jews within the rapidly-opening European society.

In 1820, the German Jewish historian Isaak Markus Jost (1793–1860) published the first serious historical work on Jews for almost two millennia, namely *The History of the Israelites*. Jost avoided the Biblical era, preferring to begin his journey with the Kingdom of Judea, and also compiled a historical narrative of different Jewish communities around the world. He realised that the Jews of his time did not form an ethnic continuum, and grasped that Israelites from place to place were rather different. Hence, he believed, there was nothing to stop Jews from total assimilation, and that in the spirit of the Enlightenment both the Germans and the Jews would turn their backs on oppressive religious institutions and form a healthy nation, based on a growing, geographically-orientated sense of belonging.

Though Jost was aware of the evolution of European nation-alism, his Jewish contemporaries were rather unhappy with his liberal, optimistic reading of the Jewish future. 'From historian Heinrich Graetz on, Jewish historians began to draw the history of Judaism as the history of a nation that had been a "kingdom", expelled into "exile", became a wandering people and ultimately turned around and went back to its birthplace.'[80]

For the German Jewish socialist philosopher Moses Hess, it was a racial struggle rather than a class struggle that would define the shape of Europe. Accordingly, he suggested, Jews should reflect on their cultural heritage and ethnic origin. For Hess, the conflict between Jews and Gentiles was the product of racial differentiation, and was thus unavoidable.

The ideological path from Hess's pseudo-scientific racist orientation to Zionist historicism is clear. If Jews are indeed an alien racial entity (as Hess, Jabotinsky and others believed), they had better seek to return to their natural homeland – *Eretz Yitzrael*. But Hass's assumed racial continuum wasn't scientifi-cally endorsed. In order to maintain the emerging fictional narrative, a mechanism for orchestrated denial had to be devised to prevent certain embarrassing facts from interfering.

The New Israelite, the Bible and Archaeology

In Palestine, the new Jews and later the Israelis were determined to recruit the Old Testament and transform it into the unifying code of the future Jewish people. The 'nationalisation' of the Bible would plant in the minds of young Jews the idea that they were the direct descendants of their great, ancient ancestors. Bearing in mind the fact that nationalisation was largely a secular movement, the Bible was stripped of its spiritual and religious meaning. Instead, it was viewed as a historical text describing a 'real' chain of events in the past.

Through their heroic ancestors, the new nationalist Jews

learned to love themselves and hate others, except this time they would possess the military might to inflict real pain on their neighbours. More worrying was the fact that instead of a super-natural entity (namely, God) to command them to invade and commit genocide against the 'Promised Land's' indigenous inhabitants, in the Jewish national revival project it was they themselves – Herzl, Jabotinsky, Weizmann, Ben-Gurion, Sharon, Peres, Barak, Netanyahu, Lieberman, etc – who would decide to expel and kill. God no longer killed in the name of the Jewish people, the Jews did. They did it with Jewish symbols decorating their planes and tanks, and followed commands issued in Hebrew, the newly restored language of their ancestors.

The Zionist hijacking of the Bible was in fact a desperate Jewish answer to German Early Romanticism. However, as much as 19th century German philosophers, poets, architects and artists were ideologically and aesthetically excited about pre-Socratic Greece, they knew very well that they were not Hellenism's (biological) sons and daughters. The Jewish nationalists took their project one step further, binding themselves into a blood chain with their mythical forefathers; Hebrew, formerly a sacred tongue, became an everyday spoken language. German Early Romantics never went that far.

German intellectuals during the nineteenth century were also fully aware of the distinction between Athens and Jerusalem. For them, Athens stood for the universal, an epic chapter of humanity and humanism. Jerusalem, on the contrary, was a grand chapter of tribal barbarism, a representation of the banal, non-universal, monotheistic, merciless God, the killer of elder and infant alike. The German Early Romantic era left us with Hegel, Nietzsche, Fichte, Heidegger and just a few Jewish self-haters, chief amongst them Weininger. No master ideological thinkers were to be found amongst the Jerusalemites. Some second-rate German Jewish scholars tried to preach Jerusalem in the Germanic exedra, amongst them Hermann Cohen, Franz Rosenzweig and Ernst

Bloch, but they apparently failed to notice that their efforts bore the traces of Jerusalem in Christianity, which German Early Romantics despised.

In their effort to resurrect 'Jerusalem', archaeology was recruited to provide the Zionist epic with its necessary 'scientific' grounding, to unify the Biblical age with the moment of revival. Arguably the most astonishing moment of this bizarre trend occurred in 1982, with the 'military burial ceremony' of the bones of Shimon Bar Kochba, a Jewish rebel who had died 2,000 years earlier. Overseen by the chief military rabbi, a televised military burial was given to a sporadic assortment of bones found in a cave near the Dead Sea. In effect, the suspected remains of a first-century figure were treated as an IDF casualty – archaeology's national role cemented the past and present, while leaving the *Galut* out.

It didn't take long before things turned the other way around. As archaeological research became more and more independent of Zionist dogma, inconvenient truths trickled out. It became impossible to ground the authenticity of Biblical tales in forensic facts. If anything, archaeology *refutes* the historicity of the Bible: the Book, according to non-Jewish scholars such as Thomas Thompson, is a 'late collection of innovative literature written by a gifted theologian'.

As Sand points out, early Biblical narrative is soaked in Philistines, Aramaic and camels. As far as excavations can enlighten us, Philistines didn't appear in the region before the twelfth century BC, Aramaic appears a century later and camels didn't show their cheerful faces before the eighth century BC. Nor has much been found in the Sinai Desert to prove the story of the legendary Egyptian exodus – apparently 3 million Hebrew men, women and children marched there for forty years without leaving a single *Mazza Ball* behind. The Biblical story of the Hebrews' resettlement in Canaan, moreover, and the genocide of the *goyim* inhabiting the Promised Land (which contemporary

Israelites imitate to such success) looks like yet another myth: Jericho, the guarded city flattened by the sound of Hebrew horns and almighty supernatural intervention, was just a tiny village during the thirteenth century BC.

Above all, Israel regards itself as the resurrection of the monumental Kingdom of David and Solomon. Yet excavation in the Old City of Jerusalem in the 1970s revealed that David's kingdom was no more than a tiny enclave. Evidence that, according to the archaeologist (and second IDF Chief of Staff) Yigal Yadin, could be traced back to King Solomon, was later refuted by forensic tests made using Carbon-14 dating.

Such scientifically verifiable facts throw Zionist researchers into confusion. The Bible is fiction, and not much in it can substantiate the glorification of the Jewish people in Palestine at any stage. It would appear, rather, to be an ideological text that is being made to serve social and political ends.

Who Invented the Jews?

Who are the Jews? Where did they come from? How is it that in different historical periods they appear in so many different and remote places?

Though most contemporary Jews are utterly convinced that their ancestors are the Biblical Israelites who were brutally exiled by the Romans, the truth is that contemporary Jews have nothing to do with these ancient Israelites, who were never even sent into exile, the Roman exile is just another Jewish myth.

Says Shlomo Sand: 'I started looking for research studies about the exile from the land, but to my astonishment I discovered that it has no literature. The reason is that no-one exiled the people of the country. The Romans did not exile peoples and they could not have done so even if they had wanted to. They did not have trains and trucks to deport entire populations. Those kind of logistics did not exist until the 20th century. From this, in effect, the whole book was born: in the realisation that Judaic society was not dispersed and was not exiled.'[81]

The thought of the Roman Imperial Navy working 24/7 to *schlep* Moishe'le and Yanke'le to Córdoba and Toledo may help Jews to feel important as well as *schleppable*, but common sense suggests the Roman armada had far more important things to do. Far more interesting is the logical conclusion: if the people of Israel were not expelled, then the real descendants of the inhabitants of the Kingdom of Judea must be the Palestinians. Sand again: 'No population remains pure over a period of thousands of years, but the chances that the Palestinians are descendants of the ancient Judaic people is much greater than the chances that you or I are its descendants. The first Zionists, up until the Arab Revolt [1936–39], knew that there had been no exiling, and that the Palestinians were descended from the inhabitants of the land. They knew that farmers don't leave until they are expelled. Even Yitzhak Ben-Zvi, the second president of the State of Israel, wrote in 1929 that, "the vast majority of the peasant farmers do not have their origins in the Arab conquerors, but rather before then, in the Jewish farmers who were numerous and a majority in the building of the land."'[82]

In his book, Sand takes this idea further, suggesting that, until the Arab Revolt, the so-called leftist Zionist leaders tended to believe that the Palestinian peasants (actually likely to be Jews by origin) would assimilate into the emerging Hebrew culture, and would eventually join the Zionist movement. Ber Borochov believed that 'a *fellah* [Palestinian peasant] dresses as a Jew, and behaves as a working-class Jew, and won't be at all different from the Jew.'[83] This notion reappeared in Ben-Gurion's and Ben-Zvi's writings. Both Zionist leaders realised that Palestinian culture was steeped in Biblical traces, linguistically as well as geographically (e.g. in the names of villages, towns, rivers and mountains). At least at that early stage, both regarded the indigenous Palestinians as ethnic relatives and potential brothers. They also regarded Islam as a friendly 'democratic religion'. After 1936, both Ben Gurion and Ben-Zvi toned down their 'multicultural' enthusiasm. As far as Ben-Gurion was concerned, ethnic cleansing of the Palestinians seemed to be far more appealing.

If the Palestinians are the 'real Jews', then, who are those people who call themselves Jews? Sand's answer is simple and sensible: 'The people did not spread, but the Jewish religion spread. Judaism was a converting religion. Contrary to popular opinion, in early Judaism there was a great thirst to convert others.'[84] Monotheistic religions, being less tolerant than polytheistic ones, have an impetus to expand. Jewish expansionism in its early days was not just similar to Christian proselytising, but it was actually Jewish expansionism that *planted* the zeal for conversion in early Christian thought and practice.

The Jews of Spain, widely believed to be blood relatives of the ancient Israelites, appear to be converted Berbers[85]. Sand says: 'I asked myself how such large Jewish communities appeared in Spain. And then I saw that Tariq ibn Ziyad, the supreme commander of the Muslims who conquered Spain, was a Berber, and most of his soldiers were Berbers. Dahia al-Kahina's Jewish Berber Kingdom had been defeated only 15 years earlier. And the truth is there are a number of Christian sources that say many of the conquerors of Spain were Jewish converts. The deep-rooted source of the large Jewish community in Spain was those Berber soldiers who converted to Judaism.'[86]

As one would expect, Sand approves of the largely accepted assumption that the Judaicised Khazars constitute the main origins of Jewish communities in Eastern Europe, which he calls the 'Yiddish Nation'. When asked why these Jews happen to speak Yiddish – largely regarded as a German medieval dialect – he answers: 'The Jews were a class of people dependent on the German bourgeoisie in the east, and thus they adopted German words.'[87]

Sand leaves us with the inevitable conclusion that contemporary Jews do not have a common origin, that their Semitic origins are a myth. Jews have no origin in Palestine whatsoever, and therefore their act of so-called 'return' must be realised as pretext for a tribal expansionist invasion.

Although Jewish-ness does not constitute any racial continuum, the Jewish identity is racially-orientated. Many Jews, even secular ones, continue to regard mixed marriage as the ultimate threat. Furthermore, in spite of modernisation and secularisation, the vast majority of secular Jews continue to enact the blood ritual of circumcision.

Unlike other 'new historians' who have tried to undermine the assumptions of Zionist historiography, 'Sand does not content himself with going back to 1948 or to the beginnings of Zionism, but rather goes back thousands of years.'[88] Unlike the 'new historians' who 'unveil' a truth known to every Palestinian toddler, i.e. the truth of being ethnically cleansed, Sand's body of work and thought may open the door to further research into the meaning of Jewish nationalism, Jewish identity and Jewish politics. Sand's critical reading of Jewish history sets the framework for further discussion of the Jewish notion of historicity and temporality. Understanding these two crucial notions will provide the intellectual key to dismantling Jewish political power and may even help Jews to redeem themselves of their very dangerous political discourse.

If Sand is correct, then the Jews, rather than being a race, comprise a collective of many people who have been hijacked by a national movement based on myths. If Jews are not a race and have nothing to do with Semitism, then 'anti-Semitism' is, categorically, an empty signifier. In other words, criticism of Jewish nationalism, Jewish lobbying and Jewish power can only be realised as a legitimate critique of ideology, politics and practice.

The ideological enemies of Israel are engaged in a bitter conflict with the state and it's supporters. Yet the issue is not just

Israel, its army or its leadership. It is actually a war against an exclusive ideology, a phantasm that has co-opted the West and, at least momentarily, diverted it from its humanist inclinations and Athenian aspirations. To fight a spirit is far more difficult than fighting people, if only because one may first have to fight its traces within oneself. If we want to fight Jerusalem, we may have to confront the Jerusalem within.

Chapter 18

From Purim to AIPAC[89]

'Jewish-ness' is a rather broad term. It refers to a culture with many faces, various distinctive groups, different beliefs, opposing political camps, different classes and diversified ethnicity. Nevertheless, the connection between the very many people who identify themselves as Jews is rather intriguing. I am attempting to trace the intellectual, spiritual and mythological collective bond that makes Jewish ideology into such a powerful political identity.

As we have seen so far, Jewish-ness is neither a racial nor an ethnic category. Nor do Jewish people form a homogenous group. Jewish-ness may be seen by some as a continuation of Judaism, I maintain that this is not necessarily the case either. Though Jewish-ness borrows some fundamental Judaic elements, 'Jewish-ness', being an ideological precept, is not 'Judaism'. It is *categorically different* from Judaism. Furthermore, as we know by now, many of those who proudly define themselves as Jews have very little knowledge of Judaism. Many of them are atheists or non-religious, and may even overtly oppose Judaism or any other religion. Many such Jews also maintain their Jewish identity, however, and are extremely proud of it. The opposition to Judaism obviously includes Zionism (at least the early version of it), but is also the basis of much of Jewish socialist anti-Zionism, as we learned earlier from examples such as Julia Bard.

What constitutes Jewish-ness? Is it a new form of religion, an ideology or just a state of mind?

If it is indeed a religion, the next questions that must be asked are: What kind of religion is it? What does this religion entail?

What do its followers believe? Is it possible to divorce oneself from it as one can step out of Christianity or Islam?

If Jewish-ness is an ideology, then the questions to ask are: What does this ideology stand for? Does it form a discourse? Is it a monolithic discourse? Does it portray a new world order? Is it aiming for peace, or for violence? Does it carry a universal message to humanity, or is it a manifestation of some tribal precepts?

If Jewish-ness is a state of mind, then the question can be raised as to whether it is rational or irrational. Does it lie within the expressible, or the inexpressible?

There is the possibility that Jewish-ness may be a strange hybrid – it can be all of those things at once (i.e. religion, ideology and state of mind). But it can also be none of these.

The Holocaust Religion

'Yeshayahu Leibowitz, the philosopher who was an observant Orthodox Jew, told me once: "The Jewish religion died 200 years ago. Now there is nothing that unifies the Jews around the world apart from the Holocaust."' *Remember What? Remember How? Uri Avnery 19.3.05*[90]

Professor Yeshayahu Leibowitz, a Latvian-born philosopher at the Hebrew University, was probably first to suggest that the Holocaust has become the new Jewish religion. The Israeli philosopher Adi Ophir also pointed out[91] that far from being merely a historical narrative, 'The Holocaust' contains numerous essential religious elements. It has priests (e.g. Simon Wiesenthal, Elie Wiesel, Deborah Lipstadt) and prophets (Shimon Peres, Binyamin Netanyahu, those who warn of the Iranian Judeocide to come). It has commandments and dogmas (e.g. 'Never Again') and rituals (memorial days, pilgrimage to Auschwitz, etc). It has an established, esoteric symbolic order (e.g. *kapos*, gas chambers, chimneys, dust, shoes, the figure of the *Musselmann*, etc). It also has a temple, Yad Vashem, and shrines – Holocaust museums – in capital cities worldwide. The Holocaust religion is also maintained by a massive global financial network, what Norman Finkelstein terms the 'Holocaust industry', as well as such institutions as the Holocaust Education Trust. This new religion is coherent enough to define its 'antichrists' (Holocaust deniers), and powerful enough to persecute them (through Holocaust-denial and hate-speech laws).

It took me many years to understand that the Holocaust, the core belief of the contemporary Jewish faith, was not an historical narrative, for historical narratives do not need the protection of the law and politicians. At a certain moment in time, a horrible chapter in the history of humanity was given an exceptionally *meta-historical* status. Its 'factuality' was sealed with draconian laws, and its reasoning secured by social and political institutions.

The Holocaust religion is, obviously, Judeo-centric to the bone. It defines the Jewish *raison d'être*. For Zionist Jews, it signifies a total fatigue of the Diaspora, and regards the *goy* as a potential irrational murderer. This new Jewish religion preaches revenge. It could well be the most sinister religion known to man, for in the name of Jewish suffering, it issues licences to kill, to flatten, to nuke, to annihilate, to loot, to ethnically cleanse. It has made vengeance into an acceptable Western value.

Critics of the notion of 'Holocaust religion' have suggested that although veneration of the Holocaust has many features characteristic of organised religion, it has not established an external deity to worship. I could not agree less: the Holocaust religion embodies the essence of the liberal democratic worldview. It offers a new form of worship, having made self-loving into a dogmatic belief in which the observant follower worships himself or herself. In the new religion, instead of old Jehovah, it is 'the Jew' whom the Jews worship: a brave and witty survivor of the ultimate genocide, who emerged from the ashes and stepped forward into a new beginning.

To a certain extent, the Holocaust religion signals the final Jewish departure from monotheism, for every Jew is potentially a little God or Goddess. Abe Foxman is the God of anti-defamation, Alan Greenspan the God of 'good economy', Milton Friedman is the God of 'free markets', Lord Goldsmith the God of the 'green light', Lord Levy the God of fundraising, Paul Wolfowitz the God of US 'moral interventionism'. AIPAC (the American–Israel Public Affairs Committee) is the American Olympus, where mortals elected in the US come to beg for mercy, forgiveness for being *Goyim* and for a bit of cash.

The Holocaust religion is the conclusive and final stage in the Jewish dialectic; it is the end of Jewish history, for it is the deepest and most sincere form of 'self-love'. Rather than requiring an abstract God to designate the Jews as the Chosen People, in the Holocaust religion the Jews cut out this divine middleman and simply choose themselves. Jewish identity politics transcends the notion of history – God is the master of ceremonies. The new Jewish God, i.e. 'the Jew', cannot be subject to any human contingent occurrence. Thus the Holocaust religion is protected by laws, while every other historical narrative is debated openly by historians, intellectuals and ordinary people. The Holocaust sets itself as an eternal truth that transcends critical discourse.

More than a few Jewish scholars in Israel and abroad accept Leibowitz's observation. Amongst them is Marc Ellis, a prominent Jewish theologian with a revealing insight into the dialectic of the new religion. 'Holocaust theology,' Ellis says, 'yields three themes that exist in dialectical tension: suffering and empowerment, innocence and redemption, specialness and normalisation.'[92]

Though the Holocaust religion has not replaced Judaism, it has given 'Jewish-ness' a new meaning. It sets a modern Jewish narrative, situating the Jewish subject within a Jewish project. It allocates to Jews a central role within their own universe. The 'sufferer' and the 'innocent' march toward 'redemption' and 'empowerment'. God is out of the game, He has been sacked, having failed in his historic mission. He wasn't there to save the Jews, after all. In the new religion 'the Jew', as the new Jewish God, redeems himself or herself.

Jewish followers of the Holocaust religion idealise the condition of their existence. They then erect a framework for a future struggle towards recognition. All three of the following Holocaust 'churches' assign the Jews a major role with some global implications:

For the Zionist followers of the new religion, the implications seem relatively durable. They are there to *schlep* the entirety of world Jewry to Zion at the expense of the indigenous Palestinian people.

For Jewish Marxists, the project is slightly more complicated. For them, redemption means building a new world order, namely a socialist haven, a world dominated by dogmatic, working-class politics in which Jews happen to be no more than just one minority amongst many.

For humanist Jews, Jews must locate themselves at the forefront of the struggle against racism, oppression and evil in general. (Though the latter sounds promising, it is in fact problematic. In our current world order, Israel and the US happen to be amongst the leading oppressors. Expecting Jews to be at the forefront of humanist struggle sets them in a fight against their brethren and their supportive superpower.)

As we can see, the Holocaust functions as an ideological interface. It provides its follower with a *logos*. On the level of the conscious, it suggests a purely analytical vision of the past and present, yet, it doesn't stop there – it also defines the struggle yet to come, a vision of a Jewish future. Nevertheless, as a consequence it fills the Jewish subject's unconscious with the ultimate anxiety: the destruction of the 'I'.

Needless to say, a body of ideas that stimulates the conscious mind (ideology) and steers the unconscious (spirit) makes a very good recipe for a winning religion. This structural bond of ideology and spirit is fundamental to the Judaic tradition. The bond between the legal clarity of the *halakha* (religious law, i.e. ideology) and the mysterious nature of Jehovah as well as the teachings of the Kabbalah (i.e. spirit) make Judaism into a totality, a universe in itself. Bolshevism – the mass movement, rather than the political theory – is built upon the very same structure, in this case the lucidity of pseudo-scientific materialism together with the fear of capitalist appetite. Neoconservative ideology is also in accordance with the same fundamental structure, locking the subject in the chasm between the alleged forensic lucidity of WMDs and the inexpressible fright of the 'terror to come'.

This bond between the conscious and unconscious brings to mind the Lacanian notion of the 'real', or that which cannot be symbolised (i.e. expressed in words). The real is the inexpressible, it is inaccessible. In Žižek's words, 'the real is impossible', 'the real is the trauma'. Nevertheless, this trauma shapes the symbolic order and forms our reality.

The Holocaust religion fits nicely into the Lacanian model. Its spiritual core is rooted deeply in the domain of the inexpressible. Its preaching teaches us to see a threat in everything. Yet, the core narrative, the trauma is sacred. It is protected, it is untouchable, very much like the dream. You can recall your dream but you cannot change it.

Interestingly enough, the Holocaust religion extends far beyond the internal Jewish discourse. In fact, it operates as a *mission*, and not only because its shrines are built far and wide, the Holocaust is now being touted as a possible pretext for nuking Iran. Both Israeli leaders and Jewish lobbyists around the world seem to be interpreting the Iranian nuclear energy project as a Judeocide in the making. Clearly, the Holocaust religion serves both right and left Jewish political discourse, but it appeals to the *goyim* as well, especially those who preach and advocate killing in the name of 'freedom', democracy and 'moral interventionism'.

To a certain extent, we are all subject to this religion; some of us are worshipers, others are just subject to its power. Those who attempt to revise Holocaust history are subject to abuse by the high priests of this religion. The Holocaust religion constitutes the Western 'real'. We are neither allowed to touch it, nor are we permitted to look into it. Very much like the ancient Israelites who were to obey their God but never question Him, we are marching into the void.

Scholars studying the Holocaust as a religion (in terms of theology, ideology and historicity) are engaged mainly with structural formulations: its meanings, rhetoric and historical interpretation. Some search for the theological dialectic (Marc Ellis), others formulate the commandments (Adi Ophir); some investigate its historical evolution, others expose its financial infrastructure (Norman Finkelstein). Most are engaged with a list of events that happened between 1933-45, however none of the Holocaust-religion scholars have expended any energy studying the role of the Holocaust within the long-standing Jewish continuum. From this point onward, I shall maintain that the Holocaust religion was well established a long time before the Final Solution (1942), well before *Kristallnacht* (1938), the Nuremberg Laws (1936) and even before Hitler was born (1889). The Holocaust religion is probably as old as the Jews themselves.

Jewish Archetypes
Jewish existence is dominated by pre-mediated fear, a phenomenon I coined earlier on as 'Pre-Traumatic Stress Syndrome' (Pre-TSS). Unlike Post-Traumatic Stress Disorder, in which stress is a direct reaction to an event that has or may have taken place in the past, the trauma sensed within the condition of Pre-TSS is founded on an imaginary episode set in a hypothetical or imaginary future – in other words, on an event that has never taken place. In Pre-TSS, the fantasy of future

terror pre-empts the conditions that shape the present reality. From an historical perspective, Pre-TSS can be realised as a self-fulfilling prophecy. The amplified fear matures into a traumatic reality.

The dialectic of fear has dominated the Jewish existence and mindset far longer than we are ready to admit. For, while Jewish ethnic leaders have exploited it politically since the early days of emancipation, it is much older than modern Jewish history. In fact, it is the heritage of the *Tanakh* (the Hebrew Bible), there to induce in Jews a pre-traumatic state. The Jewish Old Testament sets out binary frameworks: innocence/suffering and persecution/empowerment. The fear of Judeocide is entangled with Jewish spirit and culture.

The American anthropologist Glenn Bowman, who specialises in the study of exilic identities, offers a crucial insight into the subject of fear and its contribution to identity politics: 'Antagonism is fundamental to the process of fetishisation underlying identity, because one tends precisely to talk about who one is or what one is at a moment in which that being seems threatened. I begin to call myself such and such a person, or such and such a representative of an imagined community, at the moment something seems to threaten to disallow the being that the name I speak stands for. Identity terms come into usage at precisely the moment in which, for some reason, one comes to feel they signify a being or entity one has to fight to defend.'[93]

Bowman emphasises that it is *fear* that crystallises the notion of identity. However, once fear matures into a state of a collective pre-traumatic stress, identity re-forms itself.

It was the Bible that originally set the Jews in a state of Pre-TSS and initiated the fear of Judeocide, the Bible that paints the Jewish universe as a disaster waiting to happen. Increasingly, Bible scholars have come to dispute the historicity of the Scripture. For instance, Niels Lemche (in *The Canaanites and Their Land*) argues that the Bible was, for the most part, written after the Babylonian exile, and that those writings rework (and in large part invent) previous Israelite history to reflect and reiterate the experiences of those returning from the Babylonian exile.[94]

In other words, the Bible was written by home-comers, and incorporates hardcore exilic ideology into a historic narrative, very much in the manner of early Zionist ideologues who regarded assimilation as a death threat: 'The communities which aggregated under the leadership of the Yahwehist priesthood (at the time of the Babylonian exile) saw assimilation and apostasy not only as social death for themselves as Judeans but also as attempted deicide. They resolved to maintain an absolute and exclusive commitment to Yahweh who, they were sure, would lead them back to the land from which they had been expelled. They prescribed blood purity as a means of maintaining the borders of the national community, thus proscribed inter-marriage with those surrounding them. They also established a series of exclusivist rituals that set themselves off from their neighbours, and these not only included a surrogate form of temple worship but also a distinct calendar which ritualistically enabled them to exist in a different time frame than the commu-nities with which they shared space. All of these diacritical devices served to mark and maintain difference, but did not prevent them from trading with and thus being able to sustain themselves amongst the Babylonians.'[95]

The spectacular readings by Bowman and Lemche of the Bible and the Judaic narrative as a manifestation of exilic and marginal identity help explain the fact that Jewish-ness flourishes in exile, but loses its impetus once it becomes a domestic adventure. If Jewish-ness is indeed centred on an émigré collective survival ideology, it will prosper in exile. Once back in the dreamed-of homeland, the ideology melts into the void. Looking at Jewish history in this way also helps us to understand the success and failure of modern Jewish nationalism. Like Judaism, both

Zionism and Jewish 'progressive' ideologies are exilic by nature. They make some sense when considered in their pre-revolutionary era, but become totally meaningless once metamorphosis has occurred. To a certain extent, the wall with which Israel now surrounds itself symbolises a return to the exilic Jewish condition of the old European ghettos. Similarly, the Bund did survive the Soviet revolution, but became meaningless soon afterward and ceased to exist as an organic revolutionary setting.

That which maintains the Jewish collective identity is fear. As in the case of the Holocaust religion, Jewish-ness sets the fear of Judeocide at the core of the Jewish psyche, yet it also offers spiritual, ideological and pragmatic measures with which to deal with this fear.

Chapter 19

The Book of Esther

'Haman said to King Achashvairosh, "There is a nation scattered and separated among the nations [the Jews] throughout your empire. Their laws are different than everyone else's, they do not obey the king's laws, and it does not pay for the king to tolerate their existence. If it pleases the king, let a law be written that they be destroyed, and I will pay to the executors ten thousand silver Kikar-coins for the king's treasury."' *The Book of Esther, Chapter 3*

The Book of Esther is a biblical story that forms the basis for the celebration of Purim, probably the most joyously celebrated Jewish festival. The book tells of an attempted Judeocide, but also of Jews who manage to change their fate. In the *Book of Esther*, the Jews rescue themselves, and even get to mete out revenge.

It is set in the third year of the reign of the Persian king Ahasuerus (commonly identified with Xerxes I). It is a story of a palace, a conspiracy, the aforementioned attempted Judeocide and a brave and beautiful Jewish queen – Esther – who manages to save her people at the very last minute.

Ahasuerus is married to Vashti, whom he repudiates after she rejects his command to show herself off to his assembled guests during a feast. Esther is selected from amongst many candidates to be Ahasuerus's new bride. As the story progresses, Ahasuerus's prime minister, Haman, plots to have all the Jews in the Persian empire killed in revenge for a refusal by Esther's cousin Mordechai to bow to him in respect. Esther, now queen, plots with Mordechai to save the day for the Persian Jews. At the risk of endangering her own safety, Esther warns Ahasuerus of

Haman's murderous anti-Jewish plot. (As she had not disclosed her Jewish origins beforehand, the king had been unaware of them.) Haman and his sons are hanged on the fifty-cubit-high gallows he had originally built for Mordechai. As it happens, Mordechai takes Haman's place as prime minister. Ahasuerus's edict decreeing the murder of the Jews cannot be rescinded, so he issues another one allowing the Jews to take up arms and kill their enemies – which they do.

The moral of the story is clear. If Jews want to survive, they had better infiltrate the corridors of power. In light of *The Book of Esther*, Mordechai and Purim, AIPAC and the notion of 'Jewish power' appears to be an embodiment of a deep Biblical and cultural ideology.

However, here is the interesting twist. Though the story is presented as a record of actual events, the historical accuracy of the *Book of Esther* is in fact largely disputed by most modern Bible scholars. The lack of clear corroboration for any of the book's details with what is known of Persian history from classical sources has led scholars to conclude that the story is mostly or even totally fictional. In other words, the moral notwithstanding, the attempted genocide is fictional. Seemingly, the *Book of Esther* encourages its (Jewish) followers into collective Pre-TSS, making a fantasy of 'destruction' into an 'ideology of survival'. Indeed, some read the story as an allegory of quintessentially assimilated Jews, who discover that they are targets of anti-Semitism, but who are also in a position to save themselves and their fellow Jews.

Reading the Haman quotes above, while keeping Bowman in mind, the *Book of Esther* shapes an exilic identity. It sews existential stress and is a prelude to the Holocaust religion, setting the conditions that turn the Holocaust into reality. Interestingly a very similar, threatening narrative is explored in the beginning of Exodus. Again, in order to set an atmosphere of a '*Shoah* to come' and a liberation to follow, an existential fear is established:

> 'Now there arose a new king over Egypt, who knew not
> Joseph. And he said unto his people, "Behold, the people of
> the children of Israel are too many and too mighty for us;
> come, let us deal wisely with them, lest they multiply, and it
> come to pass, that, when there befalleth us any war, they also
> join themselves unto our enemies, and fight against us, and
> get them up out of the land." Therefore they did set over them
> taskmasters to afflict them with their burdens. And they built
> for Pharaoh store-cities, Pithom and Raamses.' *Exodus 8-11*

Both in Exodus and *The Book of Esther*, the author of the text
manages to predict the kind of accusations that would be leveled
against Jews for centuries to come, such as power-seeking,
tribalism and treachery. Shockingly, the text in Exodus evokes a
prophesy of the Nazi Holocaust. It depicts a reality of ethnic
cleansing, economic oppressive measures that eventually lead to
slave labour camps (*Pithom and Raamses*). Yet, in both Exodus and
the Book of Esther it is the Jews who eventually kill.

Interestingly, the *Book of Esther* (in the Hebrew version of the
Bible; six chapters were added to the Greek translation) is one of
only two books of the Bible that do not directly mention God (the
other is *Song of Songs*). As in the Holocaust religion, in the *Book of
Esther* it is the Jews who believe in *themselves*, in their own power,
in their uniqueness, sophistication, ability to conspire, ability to
take over kingdoms, ability to save themselves. The *Book of Esther*
is all about empowerment. It conveys the essence and
metaphysics of Jewish power.

From Purim to Washington

In an article titled 'A Purim Lesson: Lobbying Against Genocide,
Then and Now', Dr Rafael Medoff expounds on what he regards
as the lesson bequeathed to the Jews by Esther and Mordechai:

the art of lobbying. 'The holiday of Purim,' Medoff says, 'celebrates the successful effort by prominent Jews in the capitol [sic] of ancient Persia to prevent genocide against the Jewish people.'[96] This specific exercise of what some call 'Jewish power' (though Medoff does not use this phrase) has been carried forward, and is performed by modern emancipated Jews: 'What is not well known is that a comparable lobbying effort took place in modern times – in Washington, D.C., at the peak of the Holocaust.'[97]

Medoff explores the similarities between Esther's lobbying in Persia and her modern counterparts lobbying inside FDR's administration at the height of the Second World War: 'The Esther in 1940s Washington was Henry Morgenthau Jr., a wealthy, assimilated Jew of German descent who (as his son later put it) was anxious to be regarded as 'one hundred percent American.' Downplaying his Jewish-ness, Morgenthau gradually rose from being FDR's friend and adviser to his Treasury Secretary.'[98]

Clearly, Medoff also spotted a modern Mordechai: 'a young Zionist emissary from Jerusalem, Peter Bergson (real name: Hillel Kook) who led a series of protest campaigns to bring about U.S. rescue of Jews from Hitler. The Bergson group's newspaper ads and public rallies roused public awareness of the Holocaust – particularly when it organized over 400 rabbis to march to the front gate of the White House just before Yom Kippur in 1943.'[99]

Medoff's reading of the *Book of Esther* provides a glaring insight into the internal codes of Jewish collective survival dynamics, in which the assimilated (Esther) and the observant (Mordechai) join forces with Jewish interests on their minds. According to Medoff, the parallels to modern times are striking: 'Mordechai's pressure finally convinced Esther to go to the king; the pressure of Morgenthau's aides finally convinced him to go to the president, armed with a stinging 18-page report that they titled "Report to the Secretary on the Acquiescence of This

Government in the Murder of the Jews." Esther's lobbying succeeded. [Ahasuerus] cancelled the genocide decree and executed Haman and his henchmen. Morgenthau's lobbying also succeeded. A Bergson-initiated Congressional resolution calling for U.S. rescue action quickly passed the Senate Foreign Relations Committee – enabling Morgenthau to tell FDR that "you have either got to move very fast, or the Congress of the United States will do it for you." Ten months before election day, the last thing FDR wanted was an embarrassing public scandal over the refugee issue. Within days, Roosevelt did what the Congressional resolution sought – he issued an executive order creating the War Refugee Board, a U.S. government agency to rescue refugees from Hitler.'[100]

Doubtless Medoff sees the *Book of Esther* as a general guideline for a healthy Jewish conduct: 'The claim that nothing could be done to help Europe's Jews had been demolished by Jews who shook off their fears and spoke up for their people – in ancient Persia and in modern Washington.' In other words, Jews can and should do for themselves. This is indeed the moral of the *Book of Esther* as well as of the Holocaust religion.

What Jews should do for themselves is indeed an open question. Different Jews have different ideas. The neoconservatives believe in dragging the US and the West into an endless war against Islam. Some Jews believe that Jews should actually position themselves at the forefront of the struggle against oppression and injustice. Indeed, Jewish empowerment is just one answer among many. Yet it is a very powerful one, and dangerous when the American Jewish Committee (AJC) and AIPAC act as modern-day Mordechais and publicly engage in extensive lobbying efforts for war against Iran.

Both AIPAC and the AJC are inherently in line with the Hebrew Biblical school of thought. They follow their Biblical mentor, Mordechai. However, while the Mordechais are relatively easy to spot, the Esthers – those who act for Israel behind the scenes – are slightly more difficult to track.

Once we learn to consider Israeli lobbying within the parameters drawn by the *Book of Esther* and the Holocaust religion, we are then entitled to regard Mahmoud Ahmadinejad as the current Haman/Hitler figure. In addition to the AJC and AIPAC, President Obama's Chief of Staff Rahm Emanuel and Lord Levy are also Mordechais, Obama is obviously Ahasuerus, yet Esther can be almost anyone, from the last Neocon to Dick Cheney and beyond.

Brenner and Prinz

I have asked what Jewish-ness stands for. Though I accept the complexity of the notion of Jewish-ness, I also accept Yeshayahu Leibowitz's contribution to the subject: the Holocaust is probably the new Jewish religion. However, I also take the liberty of extending the notion of the Holocaust itself. Rather than referring merely to the *Shoah*, i.e., the Nazi Judeocide, I believe the Holocaust is actually engraved in the Jewish culture, discourse and spirit. The Holocaust is the essence of the collective Jewish Pre-TSS, which predates the *Shoah*. To be a Jew is to see a threat in every *Goy* , to be on a constant alert. To internalise the message of the *Book of Esther* is to aim for the most influential centres of hegemony, to collaborate with power and bond with rulers.

The American Jewish Marxist historian Lenni Brenner is fascinated by the collaboration between Zionists and Nazism. In his book *Zionism in the Age of Dictators*, Brenner presents an extract from a book written by Rabbi Joachim Prinz and published in 1937 after Rabbi Prinz left Germany for the US: 'Everyone in Germany knew that only the Zionists could responsibly represent the Jews in dealings with the Nazi government. We all felt sure that one day the government would arrange a round table conference with the Jews, at which – after the riots and atrocities of the revolution had passed – the new status of German Jewry could be considered. The government announced very solemnly that there was no country in the world which tried to solve the Jewish problem as seriously as did Germany. Solution of the Jewish question? It was our Zionist dream! We never denied the existence of the Jewish question! Dissimilation? It was our own appeal! ... In a statement notable for its pride and dignity, we called for a conference.'[101]

Brenner then cites extracts from a memorandum sent to the Nazi Party by the ZVfD (*Die Zionistische Vereinigung für Deutschland*, or Zionist Federation of Germany) on 21 June 1933: 'Zionism has no illusions about the difficulty of the Jewish condition, which consists above all in an abnormal occupational pattern and in the fault of an intellectual and moral posture not rooted in one's own tradition ... On the foundation of the new state, which has established the principle of race, we wish so to fit our community into the total structure so that for us too, in the sphere assigned to us, fruitful activity for the Fatherland is possible ... Our acknowledgement of Jewish nationality provides for a clear and sincere relationship to the German people and its national and racial realities. Precisely because we do not wish to falsify these fundamentals, because we, too, are against mixed marriage and are for maintaining the purity of the Jewish group ... We believe in the possibility of an honest relationship of loyalty between a group-conscious Jewry and the German state ...'[102]

Brenner doesn't approve of Prinz's point of view, nor of the Zionist initiative. Filled with loathing he writes: 'This document, a treason to the Jews of Germany, was written in standard Zionist clichés: "abnormal occupational pattern", "rootless intellectuals greatly in need of moral regeneration", etc. In it the German Zionists offered calculated collaboration between Zionism and Nazism, hallowed by the goal of a Jewish state: we shall wage no battle against thee, only against those that would resist thee.'[103]

Brenner, a Marxist and totally unfamiliar with the culture and ideology entangled with his subject matter, fails to see the obvious. Prinz and the ZVfD were not traitors, they were genuine Jews, adhering to a very Jewish cultural code. They followed the *Book of Esther*, assuming the Mordechai role. They tried to find a way to collaborate with what they correctly identified as a prominent emerging power. In 1969, Prinz confessed: 'Since the assassination of Walther Rathenau in 1922, there was no doubt in our minds that the German development would be toward an anti-Semitic totalitarian regime. When Hitler began to rise and, as he put it "awaken" the German nation to racial consciousness and racial superiority, we had no doubt that this man would sooner or later become the leader of the German nation.'[104]

Whether Brenner or anyone else likes it or not, Prinz proves his authenticity as a Jewish leader, possessing a highly developed survival 'radar' mechanism that fits perfectly well with the exilic ideology. In 1981 Brenner interviewed Prinz. Here is what he had to say about the 'collaborator' rabbi: '[Prinz] dramatically evolved in the forty-four years since he was expelled from Germany. He told me, off tape, that he soon realised that nothing he said there made sense in the US. He became an American liberal. Eventually, as head of the American Jewish Congress, he was asked to march with Martin Luther King and he did so.'

Once again, Brenner fails to see the obvious. Prinz didn't 'evolve' – he remained a genuine Jew, and an extremely clever one, a man who internalised the essence of Jewish émigré philosophy: in Germany be a German, and in the US be American. Be flexible, fit in and adopt relativistic thinking. Prinz, a devoted follower of Mordechai, realised that whatever is good for the Jews is simply good.

Listening to this invaluable interview[105], I was shocked to find out that Prinz actually presents his position eloquently. It is he rather than Brenner who provides a glimpse into Jewish ideology and its interaction with the surrounding reality. He understood the German *Volk* and its aspirations and Prinz presents his actions as a proud Jew. From his point of view, collaborating with Hitler was indeed the right thing to do. He was following Mordechai, and probably searching for an Esther as well. It is only natural that Prinz later became President of the AJC and a prominent Jewish American leader, despite his collaboration with Hitler.

Zionism vs. Exile

Once we learn to look at Jewish-ness as an exilic culture, as the embodiment of the 'ultimate other' we can understand it as a collective continuum grounded on a fantasy of horror. Jewish-ness is the materialisation of fear politics into a pragmatic agenda, as is the Holocaust religion. It is as old as the Jews themselves. Prinz could foresee the Holocaust; both Prinz and the ZVfD could anticipate a Judeocide. From a Jewish ideological point of view, they acted appropriately in collaborating. They were committed to their esoteric ethics set within an esoteric cultural discourse.

Zionism held out great promise. It could convert Jews into Israelites, and identify and fight the *Galut*, the exilic aspect of the Jewish people and culture. But Zionism was doomed to failure, for obvious reasons: within a culture metaphysically centred on exilic ideology, the last thing you can expect is a successful homecoming. In order to live out its promise, Zionism had to liberate itself from Jewish exilic ideology, and from the Holocaust religion. Yet it has failed to do this. Exilic to the bone, Zionism turned to antagonising the indigenous Palestinians in order to maintain its fetish of Jewish identity.

As it failed to divorce itself from Jewish émigré ideology, Zionism lost the opportunity to develop any form of domestic culture. Consequently, Israeli culture and politics are a strange amalgam of indecisiveness, a mixture of colonial empowerment with the *Galut's* victim mentality.

Connecting the Dots

Chapter 20

Donations, Think Tanks and Media Outlets

Following the 2010 British parliamentary election, the *Jewish Chronicle* published a list of Parliament's twenty-four Jewish MPs – twelve from the Conservatives, ten from Labour and two from the Liberal Democrats. British commentator Stuart Littlewood elaborated on these figures and presented the following analysis:

'The Jewish population in the UK is 280,000 or 0.46 per cent. There are 650 seats in the House of Commons so, as a proportion, Jewish entitlement is only three seats. With 24 seats Jews are eight times over-represented. Which means, of course, that other groups must be under-represented, including Muslims. If Muslims, for instance, were over-represented to the same extent as the Jews (i.e. eight times) they'd have 200 seats. All hell would break loose.'[106]

Why are Jews so overwhelmingly over-represented in Parliament, in British and American political pressure groups, in political fundraising and in the media? Haim Saban, the Israeli-American media mogul multibillionaire, interviewed in *The New Yorker*, offered an answer. At a conference in Israel, Saban described his formula. His 'three ways to be influential in American politics,' he said, were: make donations to political parties, establish think tanks, and control media outlets.[107]

As I have pointed out earlier on, there is no such a thing as 'Jewish conspiracy'. Everything is in the open. In front of TV cameras from all over the world, listed Israeli-propaganda author, former British Foreign Secretary David Miliband gave Israel the green light for Operation Cast Lead, suggesting in Sderot that 'Israel should, above all, seek to protect its own citizens.'[108] In practice, Miliband made all British people complicit in a colossal Israeli war crime. Miliband also pushed for an amendment of British universal jurisdiction laws just to remove the threat of Israeli politicians and generals being arrested once they landed in the UK[109]. Openly Zionist Lord Levy raised funds for the Labour Party at the time when it launched, under Prime Minister Tony Blair, a criminal war in Iraq intended in part to erase one of the last pockets of Arab resistance to Zionism. I cannot determine whether Lord Levy was involved in any political decisions, yet he, too, was not shy about his status as Tony Blair's 'No 1 fundraiser'. In the media, *Jewish Chronicle* writers David Aaronovitch and Nick Cohen enthusiastically advocated the same criminal war in the name of 'moral interventionism'. Cohen also founded the Euston Manifesto 'think tank' to support neoconservative ideologies in Britain.

Miliband, Levy, Aaronovitch and Cohen are all in line with Saban's thinking: influence, donations, think tanks, media. The Saban formula is deeply brewed in the Judaic religious tradition, and in Jewish culture and ideology. Saban's formula is informed by Mordechai – Saban internalised the true meaning of the *Book of Esther*. However, it goes further. As much as Jews are advised by some Judaic texts to bond with rulers, democracy in its current state has provided us with some very flimsy characters in leading political positions.

Zionism and Democracy

Milton Friedman admitted in the 1970's that 'free markets' are good for the Jews. Zionists and Jewish ethnic campaigners take it further – they appear to love democracy. The Jewish state claims to be 'the only democracy in the Middle East'. Israel's supporters around the world also advocate conflicts in the name of 'democracy'. Tragically enough, killing in the name of democracy is what Neocons call 'moral intervention.' Indeed, democracy is the ideal political platform for the Zionist influence merchant. Democracy today, especially in the English-speaking world, is a political system that specialises in positioning inadequate, unqualified and dubious types in leadership positions. Two such democratically elected leaders launched an illegal war in Iraq, and marched the West into financial disaster.

Running a state is not an easy task, and surely requires talent and training. In the past, our elected political leaders were experienced politicians who had achieved something in their lives, whether in academia, the financial world, industry or the military. Candidates for premiership had *curriculum vitaes* to share. Evidently this is not the case anymore. Time after time, we are left with a 'democratic choice' to give our vote to one or another laughable young failure: rising political 'stars' who have achieved little or nothing in their lives, who are unqualified to run a state. We are imprisoned by a catastrophic political system that pretends to reflect our 'free choice'.

And what qualifications did Blair or Bush possess before taking the wheel? What experience can David Cameron call upon to rescue Britain from total disaster on every front (the financial crisis, the Middle East, Afghanistan, education, the NHS and so on)? The answer is none. Our lives, our future and the future of our children are in the hands of ludicrous, clueless characters. Indeed, the 2010 election in Britain resulted in a hung Parliament, as no single leader could persuade the public that he had the talent, the integrity or even just the aura of true leader.

But here is the news: as much as our elected leaders are totally clueless, the Sabans and the Lord Levys are far from being so. They know exactly what to do, and have been doing it for three thousand years. They are the followers of Mordechai and Esther, and know how to translate the moral of Purim into British and American practice.

With Purim in mind, we may be able to suggest an answer to Littlewood's query as to why the Jews are over-represented. We are dealing here with an exilic cultural setting that preaches lobbying, influence and control. Shaping political thought is the true meaning of the *Book of Esther*. Saban, with his remarks, is either candid or foolish enough to admit this formula in public.

The absence of a *Book of Esther* at the heart of Islam or Hinduism may explain why other marginal groups in Britain are 'merely' represented adequately and proportionately in British politics and media. Moreover, it is unlikely that this situation will change anytime soon. As opposed to most minorities and marginal identities in the West, Judaism is an exilic religion and Jewish identity is a product of exilic indoctrination.

Chapter 21

Truth, History and Integrity

Back in 2007 the notorious Jewish American right-wing organization, the ADL (The Jewish Anti-Defamation League)
announced that it recognised the events in which an estimated
1.5 million Armenians were massacred as 'genocide.' The idea of
a Zionist organization being genuinely concerned, or even
slightly moved, by another people's suffering could be a
monumental transforming moment in modern Jewish political
history. Early in 2010 the ADL once again engaged with the
Armenian question. However, in 2010, it was no longer
convinced that the Armenians had suffered that much. It ended
up lobbying the American congress not to recognise the killings
of Armenians as 'genocide'.

Following the rapidly developing rift between Israel and
Turkey over the Turkish commitment to the Palestinian cause the
ADL will no doubt have to change its take again. And yet, one
question must be raised here. How is it that an event that took
place a century ago is causing such a furore? One day it is
classified as 'genocide', the next, it is demoted to an 'ordinary'
instance of one man killing another. Did an 'historical document'
suddenly pop up on Abe Foxman's desk? Are there new facts
that led to such a dramatic revision?

The ADL's behaviour is a fascinating glimpse into the notion
of Jewish history and the Jewish understanding of the past. From
a Jewish political perspective, history is foreign to any scientific
or academic method. It transcends beyond method, factuality or
truthfulness. It also repels integrity or ethics. Following Shlomo
Sand, we can argue that Jewish history is a phantasmic yet
pragmatic tale that is there to serve the interests of one people

only. It engages with the basic question of whether a given account is 'good for the Jews' or not. In practice, the decision on whether there was an Armenian genocide or not is subject to Jewish interests: is it good for the Jews, is it good for Israel?

As Sand cleverly pointed out, history is not particularly a 'Jewish thing'. As mentioned earlier, for almost two thousand years Jews were not interested in their own or anyone else's past, at least not enough to chronicle it.

Shlomo Sand's account of the 'Jewish Nation' as a fictional invention is yet to be challenged academically. The only opposition one can find is political. The dismissal of factuality or lack of commitment to truthfulness are actually symptomatic of contemporary Jewish collective ideology and identity politics. The ADL's treatment of the Armenian topic is just one example. The Zionists' dismissal of a Palestinian past and heritage is another example. Lenni Brenner's categorical failure to interpret Rabbi Prinz's inclination to collaborate with the Nazis is symptomatic. The Jewish collective and political vision of the past is inherently Judeo-centric and oblivious to any academic or scientific procedure.

When I was young and naïve I regarded history as a serious, academic matter. As I understood it, history had something to do with truth-seeking, documents, chronology and facts. I was convinced that history aimed to convey a sensible account of the past based on methodical research. I also believed that an understanding of the past could throw some light over our present and even help us to shape a better future.

I grew up in the Jewish state and it took me a while to understand that the Jewish historical narrative is very different. In the Jewish intellectual insular world, one first decides what the historic moral is, then one invents 'a past' to fit.

When I was young, I didn't think that history was a matter of political decisions or agreements between a one Zionist lobby and another. I regarded historians as scholars who engaged in research following strict procedures. When I was young I even considered becoming an historian.

In my formative years I blindly accepted every thing they told us about our 'collective' Jewish past: the Kingdom of David, Massada, and then the Holocaust: the soap, the lampshade, the death march and the six million.

It took me many years to understand that the Holocaust, the core belief of the contemporary Jewish faith, was not at all an historical narrative, freely debated by historians, intellectuals and ordinary people. As I mentioned before, historical narratives do not need the protection of the law and political lobbies. It took me years to grasp that my great-grandmother wasn't made into a 'soap' or a 'lampshade' as I was taught in Israel. She probably perished of exhaustion, typhus or maybe even by mass shooting. This was indeed bad and tragic, but not that different from the fate of many millions of Ukrainians, on learning the real meaning of communism.

The fate of my great-grandmother was not so different from hundreds of thousands of German civilians who died in deliberate, indiscriminate bombing, just because they were Germans. Similarly, the people in Hiroshima, who died just because they were Japanese. Three million Vietnamese died just because they were Vietnamese and 1.3 million Iraqis died because they were Iraqis.

I think that 65 years after the liberation of Auschwitz, we must be entitled to start asking questions. We should ask for historical evidence and arguments rather than follow a religious narrative that is sustained by political pressure and laws. We should strip the Holocaust of its Judeo-centric exceptional status and treat it as an historical chapter that belongs to a certain time and place. The Holocaust, like every other historical narrative, must be analysed properly.

65 years after the liberation of Auschwitz we should be able to ask – why? Why were the Jews hated? Why did European people

stand up against their neighbours? Why are the Jews hated in the Middle East, surely they had a chance to open a new page in their troubled history? If they genuinely planned to do so, as the early Zionists claimed, why did they fail? Why did America tighten its immigration laws amid the growing danger to European Jews? We should also ask what purpose Holocaust denial laws serve? What is the Holocaust religion there to conceal? As long as we fail to ask questions, we will be subjected to Zionist lobbies and their plots. We will continue killing in the name of Jewish suffering. We will maintain our complicity in Western imperialist crimes.

Chapter 22

Being in Time

One may be left perplexed on learning that just three years after the liberation of Auschwitz (1945) the newly-formed Jewish state ethnically cleansed the vast majority of the indigenous population of Palestine (1948). Just five years after the end of World War Two, the Jewish state brought to life racially-discriminatory return laws in order to prevent the 1948 Palestinian refugees from coming back to their cities, villages, fields and orchards. These laws, still in place today, were not categorically different from the notorious Nazi Nuremberg Laws.

This unique institutional lack of compassion deserves some attention. One might expect the victims of oppression and discrimination to locate themselves at the forefront of the battle against evil. One might expect the victims of oppression and discrimination to not visit the same fate on others. This expectation never happened as far as the Jewish State is concerned. With millions of besieged Palestinians, Israel has given itself the reputation of a pariah state.

How is it that the Jewish political and ideological discourse fails so badly to draw the obvious and necessary lesson from history and Jewish history in particular? How is it that in spite of 'Jewish history' appearing to be an endless tale of Jewish suffering, Israel and its lobbies are so blind to any form of ethical or universal thinking? How is it that, in spite of the Holocaust, Israel and Jewish lobbies invest so much energy in evoking hatred towards enemies of Israel and world Jewry?

As we have discussed, within the context of Jewish identity politics and Ideology, history doesn't play a guiding role.

As Sand noted, instead of history, the Torah provided

Rabbinical Judaism with a spiritually-driven plot. It conveyed an image of purpose and fate. However, things changed in the 19th century. Due to the rapid emancipation of European Jewry together with the rise of nationalism and the spirit of Enlightenment, assimilated European Jews felt bound to redefine their beginning in secular, national and rational terms. This is when Jews 'invented' themselves as 'people' and as a 'class'. Like other European nations Jews felt the urge to posses a coherent narrative.

Inventing history is not exactly a crime – people, organisations and nations often do it. Yet, in spite of the rapid process of assimilation, Jewish secular ideology and politics failed to encompass the real meaning of historical thought. Indeed, the assimilated secular Jews was very successful in dropping God, they managed also to drop their symbolic identifiers such as the skullcap and the *kaftan*. And yet, the assimilated Jews failed to replace divinity with an alternative anthropocentric ethical and metaphysical realisation.

The newly-born Jewish political identity was, indeed, quick to invent history. Yet, not a single Jewish attempt to replace God with a Jewish secular anthropocentric moral system has been noted[110]. In short, when Jewish secular humanists are preaching to us in the name of 'Jewish values' we had better challenge them and verify what values they are referring to.

Temporality

I only recently understood that the Jewish secular project is not only foreign to history and ethical thinking, it is actually detached from the notion of temporality.

Temporality is inherent to the human condition. 'To be' is 'to be in time'. We are hung between the past that is drifting away into the void and the unknown that proceeds towards us from the future. Through the present, the so-called 'here and now', we meditate on that which is past, and hope for forgiveness. Ethics, as reflected by Kant's categorical imperative, is also bound up with temporality: 'act only according to that maxim whereby you can at the same time will that it should become a universal law'. Kant reviews the moral act in respect to its temporal perspective. The universal law is looked upon from the perspective of the future and past. Ethics and temporality can be seen as an endless dialogue between 'yesterday' and 'tomorrow'.

The present should be understood as a creative dynamic mode where past premeditates its future. But far more crucially, it is also where the imaginary future can re-write its past. I will try to elucidate this idea through a simple and hypothetical yet horrifying war scenario. We, for instance, can envisage an horrific situation in which an Israeli so-called 'pre-emptive' nuclear attack on Iran escalates into a disastrous nuclear war, in which tens of millions of people perish. I guess that amongst the survivors of such a nightmare scenario, some may be bold enough to argue that 'Hitler might have been right after all.'

The above is obviously a fictional scenario, and by no means a wishful one, yet such a vision of a 'possible' horrific development should restrain Israeli or Zionist aggression towards Iran. As we know, Israeli officials threaten to flatten Iran rather too often. In practice, pre-TSS Israelis make this devastating scenario into a possible reality.

Seemingly, Israelis and Zionist politicians fail to see their own actions in the light of history. They fail to look at their actions in terms of their consequences. From an ethical perspective, the above 'imaginary' scenario is there to prevent Israel from attacking Iran. Yet, as we all know, Israel and its lobbies are desperate to dismantle the so-called 'Iranian threat'. My explanation is simple. The Jewish state and the Jewish discourse in general are completely foreign to the notion of temporality. Israel is blinded to the consequences of its actions, it only thinks of its actions in terms of short-term pragmatism. Instead of temporality, Israel thinks in terms of an extended present.

Grasping the notion of temporality is the ability to accept that the past is shaped and revised in the light of a search for meaning. History, and historical thinking, are the capacity to rethink the past and the future.

To a certain extent, history revisionism is the true essence of historical thinking for it reshapes the past through an imaginary future perspective and vice versa. Revisionism is imbued in the deepest possible understanding of temporality, and therefore inherent to humanity and humanism. It is obvious that those who oppose historical revisionism are, in practice, operating against the foundations of humanism.

This philosophical outlook is not very flattering to Jewish discourse and identity politics. Jewish ideology and political discourse openly opposes revision and revisionism. Similar to the Judaic precept, Jewish politics is there to fix and cement a narrative and terminology, and it would oppose any historical revision or reformism. The Zionist ideology presents itself as a historical narrative, and it took me many years to grasp that Zionism, Jewish identity politics and ideology were actually crude, blunt assaults on history, the notion of history and temporality. In fact, Jewish national politics is an attempt to place the people of Israel beyond historical temporality. Once the Jewish past is cemented and sealed, the fate and the operative actions can be deduced: from a Zionist prospective, the Diaspora Jews should adhere to and support the homecoming project, the Palestinian people should clear the space, Western superpowers should finance it all, and so on. Such a vision alienates its followers from temporality and ethics. Those who still insist on criticising the validity of the Zionist argument are silenced. Those who follow the Zionist and Jewish political philosophy are doomed to drift away from humanism and humanity.

Such an explanation starts to throw light on Israeli conduct and Jewish support for Israeli war crimes.

Inventing a past is not the most worrying issue when it comes to Israel and Zionism. As I mentioned before, people and nations do tend to invent their past. However, celebrating one's phantasmic past at the expense of the other is obviously an ethical issue, and in the case of Israel the problem goes deeper. It is the attempt to seal yesterday that led to the collective ethical collapse of Israel and its supporting crowd. Instead of a celebration of life through transformation of meanings, Zionism was there to promise redemption via a blind acceptance of a single narrative. It promised to bring the 'wandering' to an end. It promised to bring about a 'new Jew', a civilised being, an ethical character. Establishing a fictitious, unchangeable past, Zionism aimed to deliver the Jews an eternal redemption through an exclusivist and racially-oriented homecoming project. Jewish politics in general and Zionism in particular should be realised as attempts to place the people of Israel beyond temporality. The Marxist East European Bund invented the 'Yiddish Nation' that was supposed to save the Jews via the communist revolution, Zionism invented Jewish exile in order to create the pretext for 'homecoming'. Once the Jewish past is cemented and revision is prohibited, the Jewish fate becomes a matter of logical deduction. This is also when compassion and ethics evaporate.

The dismissal of temporality, the lack of capacity to reflect upon oneself from the futuristic perspective, explains the Israeli collective complicity in some of their horrendous war crimes. This should be enough to explain why the Israelis sliced up the Holy Land with separation walls and barbed wires. It explains why Israelis drop White Phosphorous on their next-door neighbours as they seek shelter in a UN shelter. It also explains why Israeli Navy Seal commandos ended up executing peace activists on the Mavi Marmara on the high seas. It also explains why newly-born Israel was quick to expel the vast majority of the Palestinian indigenous population just three years after the liberation of Auschwitz. These events have nothing to do with the colonialist nature of the Jewish state as some Marxist ideologists insist. They may have something to do with the racist, supremacist, chauvinist ideology that fuels Zionism, and must be grasped in philosophical and metaphysical terms. We are not talking here about sociology, psychology or material determinism, we are actually searching for categorical understanding.

People who defy the true meaning of history are alienated from temporality. People who cannot revise their past are doomed to fail to comprehend the notion of consequence, causality and ethics. People who defy history never look in the mirror. They are doomed to think that anti-Semitism is an 'irrational' social phenomenon that erupts 'out of nowhere'. Accordingly they must believe that the *Goyim* are potentially mad. Bear in mind that the Goyim are the vast majority of the human population.

That which is called 'Jewish history', is actually a relentless attempt to narrate the past from the point in time where Jewish pain is detected. I would argue that the appropriate temporal approach would be to ask what is it that brought so much hatred on the people of Israel. I would even take it further and ask, is there anything that we know nowadays about Jewish culture that may help us to understand the Jewish past and Jewish suffering? Can Israeli behaviour throw light on the events that led to the Holocaust, or other instances of persecution of Jews?

The relentless clinging to a phantasmic, invented yesterday is there to provide the false and very misleading impression that the tomorrow can be also determined. Seemingly, by the means of self-imposed blindness, Israel has led itself into an inevitable disaster. Clearly, Zionism failed to answer the Jewish question. Yet it may be that the conditions created by enlightenment, liberalism and emancipation cannot be easily addressed by any form of Jewish political collectivism except orthodoxy, which is pretty much impervious to enlightenment, liberalism, individualism and emancipation all together. If this is indeed the case, Jewish secular collectivism is disastrous. As we come to the end of this text, it seems as though the Third Category's political, ideological and identity discourse cannot be sustained.

However, Israel is not alone. As tragic as it appears to be, America and Britain have managed to willingly give up on temporality. It is the lack of true historical discourse that stopped Britain and America from understanding their future, present and past. As in the case of Jewish history, American and British politicians insist on a banal and simplistic historic tale to do with WWII, Cold War, Islam, 911 etc. Tragically, the criminal Anglo-American genocide in Iraq and Afghanistan, AKA 'The War against Terror', is a continuation of our self-inflicted blindness. Since Britain and America failed to grasp the necessary message from the massacres in Hamburg and Dresden, Nagasaki and Hiroshima, there was nothing that could stop English-speaking imperialism from committing similar crimes in Korea, Vietnam, Afghanistan and Iraq. Similarly, both Britain and America were caught completely unprepared for regional *Intifada* in the Middle East and North Africa. Western estrangement has taken its toll. Western political leadership is totally detached from humanist thinking or judgments that involve ethics.

For America, Britain and the West to rescue themselves all they have to do is to revert to Western values of ethics and openness. They must drift away from Jerusalem and reinstate the spirit of Athens.

Closure

It is my hope that this book will throw some light on questions to do with Jewish-ness and Jewish ideology, identity and politics. Having thought and written about this topic for over a decade, and looking back over my work, I realise that it was actually the Jewish 'anti-Zionists' who taught me more about Zionism, Jewish nationalism and tribalism than any rabid Zionist or Israeli nationalist.

While both Zionism and Jewish socialism are full of inconsistencies, Zionism can be realised as an attempt to resolve the abnormality in the Jewish condition. The so-called Jewish progressive discourse, on the other hand, is an attempt to shove ideological inconsistencies and discrepancies (largely tribalism vs. universalism) under the carpet.

As much as this book explores different aspects of Jewish political neurosis, and may help to untangle the bond between Israel and Jews across the world, it fails to answer one question: what do modern emancipated Jews want? Considering the energy and resources that Jewish lobbies pour into political parties around the world, and the efforts undertaken to influence media and leadership, it is far from clear what the Lord Levys and the Haim Sabans are trying to achieve. They spend a lot of money but what are they trying to buy? What is Israel itself trying to achieve? The more influence Jewish and Israeli lobbies gain, the greater resentment Jews earn. Is it 'security' that they seek, as they say? I really do not think so.

One answer may be that Jews do not agree amongst themselves about what is right for the Jews. Back in 2003, Zionists believed, for instance, that sending the US and Britain to destroy Iraq was 'good for the Jews'. Jewish anti-Zionists were convinced that opposing the same war 'as Jews' was the best thing Jews could do for themselves. The Jewish escapists were and are still convinced that turning a blind eye is the best thing for the Jews.

Whether Jews know or can agree on what is 'good for the Jews' is an open question, yet to identify politically as a Jew and to wonder what is 'good for the Jews' is the true essence of Jewish *tribal thinking* and the Third Category identity. This is where I began this book, and this, apparently, is where I end it.

Epilogue

I would love to end this book on a positive note, to suggest a practical solution. That it is not easy. Jewish cultural and ideological exceptionalism has left Jewish political discourse with no hope or future.

As a young Israeli I believed in the Zionist ethos, I regarded myself as an inherent part of the Jewish modern revival project. I saw myself as part of Jewish history, and Jewish history as an extension of myself. As a young Israeli growing up in the post-1967 era, I saw myself and the people around me as an evolving collective consciousness, fighting a revolutionary battle for historic justice.

It took a while before I realised that my historical revival project was in fact a chain of blind spots. It took me many years to understand that I myself was a black spot. I remember my high school class visit to *Yad Vashem*, the Israeli Holocaust Museum in Jerusalem located next to *Deir Yassin*, a Palestinian village that was wiped of its inhabitants in 1948. I was fourteen years old at the time. I asked the emotional tour guide if she could explain the fact that so many Europeans loathed the Jews so much and in so many places at once. I was thrown out of school for a week. It seems I didn't learn the necessary lesson because when we studied the middle age blood libels, I again wondered out loud how the teacher could know that these accusations of Jews making *Matza* out of young Goyim's blood were indeed empty or groundless. Once again I was sent home for a week. In my teens I spent most of my mornings at home rather than in the classroom.

As much as I was a sceptic youngster, I was also horrified by the Holocaust. In the 1970s Holocaust survivors were part of our social landscape. They were our neighbours, we met them in our family gatherings, in the classroom, in politics, in the corner shop. They were part of our lives. The dark numbers tattooed on their white arms never faded away. It always had a chilling effect. Yet I must mention that I can hardly recall a single Holocaust survivor who ever attempted to manipulate me emotionally. Recently I spoke to a Scottish friend who volunteered in a Kibbutz in the 1970s. That Kibbutz was known for its high percentage of Holocaust survivors. My Scottish friend pointed out to me that he really enjoyed his time there working and talking with those survivors. They were largely very quiet and polite, they never used their past as a claim for fame. It was the young Israelis who he couldn't stand. My experience was very similar – as far as my personal experience is concerned, it is always the alleged sons, daughters and grandchildren of survivors who exploit the Holocaust as a political argument, or a claim for some form of exceptionalism.

The American historian Norman Finkelstein is correct when arguing that Israel transformed the Holocaust into a political tool after 1967, when it needed an 'ethical' excuse as a non-ethical occupier. I must admit that, even as a nationalist youngster, I never felt comfortable with the Holocaust. At the time I thought that Jews shouldn't brag so much about being resented.

It was actually the internalisation of the meaning of the Holocaust that transformed me into a strong opponent of Israel and Jewish-ness. It is the Holocaust that eventually made me a devoted supporter of Palestinian rights, resistance and the Palestinian right of return. In 1984, while being a soldier, during that short visit to Anzar concentration camp in Lebanon, I realized that I was on the wrong side.

It has been pointed out to me that my critical take on Zionism can be also seen as a great Zionist achievement, for Zionism vowed to create a 'free', rational, liberal and open Jewish discourse. Indeed, like an Israeli, I do not hold back, I do not mince my words either. As if this is not enough, it is no secret that I look like an Israeli and sound like one. It may well be that these are necessary qualities needed to grasp the Israeli mind, politics, identity and culture. Amongst the most productive critical voices of Israel and Jewish-ness you will find Israelis and ex-Israelis such as Israel Shahak, Israel Shamir, Gideon Levi, Shimon Tzabar, Shlomo Sand, Avrum Burg, Amira Hass, Uri Avnery, Tali Fachima, Mordechi Vannunu, Nurit Peled and a few others. I guess that there must be something positive in the Zionist heritage if it has managed to bring forth so many critical voices. Israeli media constantly tries to engage me in debate. It would seem that there is still an element of openness within the Zionist discourse.

As a young secular Israeli Jew, I believed enthusiastically in the possibility of transformation of the Jewish character into a 'civilised, authentic humanist collective'. I believed myself to be one. I then grasped, through a long and painful process that Israel wouldn't bring about a humanist Jew. It was entangled in a colossal sin and it was far too arrogant to save itself from its doomed circumstances. I realised that if I was genuinely enthusiastic about the Goyim lifestyle, I had better just leave Israel behind, dwell amongst the Goyim and even try to become one myself. So I did. To date, I have never looked back with yearning. I even proudly own the few contradictions I have managed to retain.

I guess that leaving this book without a quest for peace and reconciliation would be a missed opportunity. Needless to say, I am not holding my breath for a solution from any 'peace talks'.

Imagine an Israeli PM wakes up one sunny morning with the unusual determination to bring about true peace. In the wee small hours, wisdom embraces him or her. He or she realises that Israel is in fact Palestine: it is stretched over historic Palestine at the expense of the Palestinian people, their livelihood and their history. He or she grasps that the Palestinians are the indigenous people of the land, and the rockets they shoot from time to time are nothing but love letters to their stolen villages, orchards, vineyards and fields. Our imaginary Israeli PM realises that the so-called Israeli-Palestinian conflict can be resolved in 25 minutes once both people decide to live together. Following the Israeli unilateral tradition, an immediate televised press conference is called on the same day at 14:00. Captivated by true righteousness, the PM announces to the world and his/her people 'Israel realises its unique circumstances and its responsibility for world peace. Israel calls the Palestinian people to return to their homes. The Jewish state is to become a state of its citisens, where all people enjoy full equal rights'.

Though shocked by the sudden Israeli move, political analysts around the world would be quick to realise that, considering Israel is the representative of world Jewry, such a simple peaceful initiative won't just resolve the conflict in the Middle East, it would also bring to an end two millennia of mutual suspicion and resentfulness between Christians and Jews. Some right-wing Israeli academics, ideologists and politicians join the revolutionary initiative and declare that such a heroic unilateral Israeli act could be the one and only total and comprehensive fulfilment of the Zionist dream, for not only have Jews returned to their alleged historical home, they also have managed, at last, to love their neighbours and be loved in return.

As much as such an idea is thrilling, we shouldn't expect it to happen any time soon, for Israel is the Jewish state and Jewishness is an ethno-centric ideology driven by exclusiveness, exceptionalism, racial supremacy and a deep inherent inclination toward segregation.

For Israel and Israelis to become people like other people, all traces of Jewish ideological superiority must be eliminated first. For the Jewish state to lead a peace initiative, Israel must be de-Zionised – it should first stop being the Jewish State. Similarly, in order for an imaginary Israeli PM to bring peace about, he or she must be de-Zionised first.

As things stand, the Jewish State is categorically unable to lead the region into reconciliation. It lacks the necessary ingredients needed to think in terms of harmony and reconciliation.

The only people who can bring peace about are the Palestinians, because Palestine, against all odds and in spite of the endless suffering, humiliation and oppression, is still an ethically-driven ecumenical society.

As far as Jews are concerned, a few questions remain. Can the Jewish identity discourse be liberated from its self-imposed ideological and spiritual tyranny? Can Jewish politics drift away from supremacy? Can Jews save themselves? My answer is simple: for Jewish ideology to universalise itself and for Jews to move on and emancipate themselves, a vigorous and honest process of self-reflection must take place. Whether Jews can engage in such a critical endeavour is an open question. I don't know the answer, I guess that some can, others can't. I would hope, though, that this book may offer a fairly good start.

Acknowledgments

In particular I would like to express my gratitude to my mother Ariella who is not just intellectually inspiring but also one of my closest friends, to my wife Tali and my kids Mai and Yann who debated and challenged my thoughts throughout these years and yet supported me and my strange life-style all along. I would like to mention Mary Rizzo who was my dedicated editor for many years and contributed many great titles to my texts including the title of this book.

I would like to thank all the people who supported me, my writing and my enterprise all those years. When tsunamis of malicious slander were about to wash my shore, I came to know battalions of vibrant ethically driven individuals who stood by my side and paved the way for a journey that led eventually to the publication of this book.

I would like to thank all those journals, magazines, editors, academics, promoters, friends and activists who stood up firmly against all odds and kept publishing my writing, invited me to perform and debate my views. I would also like to express my gratitude to those who welcomed my enterprise and provided me with many inspiring insights and warm support: Gregory Mario Whitfield, Alan Hart, Paul de Rooij, Ramzy Baroud, Gill Kaffash, Ken O'keefe, Manuel Talens, Nahida Yassin, Roy Ratcliffe, Fausto Guidice, Kristoffer Larsson, Laura Susijn, Jeff Blankfort, Amelia Tucker, Sameh Habeed, Nadya Shah, Tim King, Louis Charalambous, Alexander Cockburn, Jeffrey St. Clair, Eric Walberg, Kevin Barrett, Paul J. Balles, Shahram Vahdany, Axel Reiserer, Silvia Cattori, Evelyn Hecht-Galinski, Amos Zukerman, Anthony Lawson, Gordon Duff, Francis Clark Lowes, Chris Cook, David Alpin, Gabi Weber, Massoud Nayeri, Mamoon Alabbasi, James Petras, Glenn Bowman, Eddie Hick, Paul Eisen, Lauren Booth, William W. Cook, Paul Larudee, Mohamed El

Dufani, Richard Falk, Janet Kobren, Mitch Albert, Ben Bastin, Jason Bosh, Jeff Salamt, June Terpstra, John Mearsheimer, Richard Sharma and many others. A special thanks to my friend and collaborator Sarah Gillespie who found herself discussing Jewish identity politics matters over thousands of miles on the way to concerts and recording studios.

I cannot let this opportunity pass without thanking from the bottom of my heart my half the dozen Jewish Marxist detractors who have been stalking me and my music career day and night for years, without whom I would never have grasped the real depth of tribal ferocity. It is these so called 'anti Zionist' Jewish ethnic activists who taught me more than any rabid Zionist about the true devastating practical meaning of Jewish identity politics.

Endnotes

1. Vladimir Ze'ev Jabotinsky was the founder of Zionist revisionism, author, orator and soldier. Ze'ev Jabotinsky's legacy is carried on today by Israel's Herut party (merged with other right wing parties to form the Likud in 1973) and the Betar Zionist youth movement.

2. 'The primacy of the ear' may echo (for some) the Judaic *Sh'ma Yisrael* prayer: 'Hear, O Israel: the Lord is our God, the Lord is one,' (Deuteronomy 6:4). Though Judaism allocates great importance to the act of 'hearing', it is crucial to make a clear distinction between my own call for a personal and critical judgment, as opposed to Judaic call for total obedience.

3. In spite of some disturbing Judaic thoughts that are explored in the Torah and especially in the Talmud, it is an accepted fact that the ultra-orthodox Torah Jews stand collectively against Zionism and in support of the Palestinians.

4. By Way of Deception, Victor Ostrovsky , St. Martin's, 1990 pg 86-7

5. Paul Dundes Wolfowitz (born December 22, 1943) is a leading Neoconservative, a former U.S. Deputy Secretary of Defense. As Deputy Secretary of Defense, Wolfowitz was a major architect of President Bush's Iraq policy.

6. Rahm Israel Emanuel (born November 29, 1959), former White House Chief of Staff to President Barack Obama; served as Senior Advisor to President Bill Clinton from 1993 to 1998.

7. Michael Abraham Levy (born 11 July 1944) was the chief fundraiser for the UK Labour Party. A long-standing friend of former Prime Minister, Tony Blair, Lord Levy spent nine years from 1998 as Tony Blair's special envoy to the Middle East.

8. David Aaronovitch (born 8 July 1954) is a British author,

broadcaster, and journalist. He is a regular columnist for The Times and the Jewish Chronicle. Aaronovitch was amongst the few advocates of the 2nd Iraq War within British Press.

9. Ibid pg 87

10. Jonathan Jay Pollard (born August 7, 1954) was a USA former CIA and USA's Navy employee who was convicted of spying for Israel. He received a life sentence in 1987.

11. http://www.washington-report.org/backissues/0195/9501017.htm

12. ADL-The Anti-Defamation League is a Zionist organization based in the USA. Describing itself as 'the nation's premier civil rights/human relations agency.'

13. Bernard Lawrence Madoff (born April 29, 1938) is a former American stockbroker and formerly non-executive chairman of the NASDAQ stock market. Madoff was sentenced to life in prison for his involvement in what has been described as the largest Ponzi scheme in the history of the world.

14. 'Organism' can be described as a whole hierarchical assemblage of systems made of collections of organs. While the organism functions as a whole, the particular organ fulfills an elementary function without being aware of its specific role within the entire system.

15. Appeared in the amended text (16/41992) that followed the embarrassing earlier New York Times leak.

16. Home page of the Project for the New American Century: http://www.newamericancentury.org/ (http://www.newamericancentury.org/)

17. Ibid

18. On June 3 1997 the PNAC released its 'Statement of Principles', a list of ideas that set the USA as a global police force, the guardian of 'morality', the disseminator of 'democracy' and a defender of Jewish state and its interests:
  * we need to increase defense spending significantly if we are to carry out our global responsibilities today and modernize

our armed forces for the future;

* we need to strengthen our ties to democratic allies and to challenge regimes hostile to our interests and values;

* we need to promote the cause of political and economic freedom abroad; [and]

* we need to accept responsibility for America's unique role in preserving and extending an international order friendly to our security, our prosperity, and our principles.

19. http://hubpages.com/hub/Nathan_Rotschild_and_the_Battle _Of_Waterloo

20. Jacob Schiff (the head of Kuhn, Loeb & Company) is credited with giving twenty million dollars to the Bolshevik revolution. A year after his death the Bolsheviks deposited over six hundred million rubles in Schiff's banking firm Kuhn, Loeb. (New York Journal American 1949. February 3.) One may mistakenly assume that the shift of world Jewry lobbying from Germany to America is the product of Hitler's rise. In fact the Israeli author Amos Elon (The Pity of it All) provides inter-esting historical insight into the subject. Seemingly, upon the eve of the first war, some very powerful Jewish German lobbies were operating in America. Apparently, prominent German American Jews protested against America joining England and France. In a statement to the New York Times on November 22 1914, Jacob H Schiff, head of Khun, Loeb (at the time the second largest private bank in the USA), charged the British and French with attempting to destroy Germany for reasons of trade (Elon, pg. 253). East European Jews who emigrated to the USA, evading the anti-Semitic Czarist Russia, regarded the German army as a liberator. American Jewry was mainly pro-German. The British Government took these developments seriously. The British Ambassador to the United States suspected a Jewish conspiracy in America. The 1917 Balfour Declaration was largely an attempt to divert the anti-English feelings amongst World Jewry. This strategy was

successful at least in the short-term. Following the declaration, world Jewry, both Zionists and non-Zionists, largely
embraced the side of the Allies.

21. Remarks by Chairman Alan Greenspan, Consumer Finance at
the Federal Reserve System's Fourth Annual Community
Affairs Research Conference, Washington, D.C. April 8, 2005
http://www.federalreserve.gov/boarddocs/speeches/2005/200
50408/default.htm

22. Becoming an indistinguishable part of a group or community

23. Becoming accepted within a larger group or community

24. http://www.msu.edu/~womyn/alternative.html

25. The exposure of Jews in influential positions is done in
various ways. Jewish media outlets often expose the Jewish
roots of leading key players in politics, business and media.
For instance the Jewish Chronicle in the UK names Jews in
politics and business. The Jewish Virtual Library proudly
names the Jews in different American administrations
(http://www.jewishvirtuallibrary.org/jsource/US-Israel/
bushjews.html). And if anyone wants to verify the Jewish
identity of a celebrity, there is the website http://www.
jewornotjew.com.

26. Max Simon Nordau (July 29, 1849 - January 23, 1923) was a
Zionist leader, physician, author, and social critic. Nordau
was a co-founder of the World Zionist Organization together
with Theodor Herzl.

27. Max Nordau, address at the first Zionist Congress, Basle, 1897

28. Blatant Lesbianism, 1978 Sydney Magazine. P.10-13

29. Guardian, 13 May 2000.

30. 'Women, Wimmin, Womyn, Womin, Whippets – On Lesbian
Separatism', Julie McCrossin, http://www.takver.com/history
/womyn.htm.

31. In his book, *Ben Gurion's Scandals: How the Haganah & the
Mossad Eliminated Jews*, Naeim Giladi discusses the crimes
committed by Zionists in their frenzy to import raw Jewish

labor from Iraq in the early 1950s. Giladi tells a story of a Zionist attempt to hurt Iraqi Jews in order to disseminate the Zionist message. 'In attempts to portray the Iraqis as anti-American and to terrorize the Jews, the Zionists planted bombs in the U.S. Information Service library and in synagogues. Soon leaflets began to appear urging Jews to flee to Israel.'

(http://www.bintjbeil.com/E/occupation/ameu_iraqjews.html)

32. Israelis are fascinated by the 1967 images of IDF paratroopers, the ultimate *Sabras,* sobbing in proximity to the wailing wall once they completed the invasion of Jerusalem old city. The images symbolically juxtapose the 1967 heroic military affair with the deeply emotional, humane characteristic of the *Sabra.*

33. Tzitzit - specially knotted ritual fringes worn by observant Jewish males. Tzitzit are attached to the four corners of the *Tallit* (prayer shawl)

34. The negation of the Diaspora is a central assumption in earlier Zionist trends. It is there to reject the feasibility of Jewish emancipation, integration and assimilation in the Diaspora.

35. Trials of The Diaspora, Anthony Julius pg Xl, Oxford University Press.

36. http://www.marxists.de/middleast/brenner/ch02.htm#n10

37. http://www.marxists.de/middleast/brenner/ch02.htm#n10

38. http://www.angelfire.com/il2/borochov/eco.html

39. http://www.geocities.com/Vienna/6640/zion/nordau.html

40. http://www.geocities.com/Vienna/6640/zion/jewishproblem .html

41. Franz Rosenzweig – (December 25, 1886-December 10, 1929) was a German-Jewish theologian and philosopher

42. Hermann Cohen – (4 July 1842-4 April 1918) was a German-Jewish philosopher. Cohen is regarded by some as the most prominent 19th century Jewish philosopher.

43. Gershom Scholem (December 5, 1897-February 21, 1982), was a German-born Jewish philosopher and historian. Scholem is

widely regarded as the founder of the modern, academic study of Kabbalah and Jewish Mysticism.

44. Gefilte fish – a Jewish Ashkenazi fish dish. Typically eaten on Sabbath and religious holidays.

45. Women Against Fundamentalism and the Jewish community *Journal no.4 1992/1993. pp.3-5*

46. Unlike Christianity and Islam, Judaism is a non-reformist religion. In Judaism there is no room for even minor modifications. Judaism is a sealed list of 613 commandments (*Mitzvas*) that must be followed strictly. From a Judaic (i.e. religious) point of view, to depart from Judaism is, in practice, to form a new Church. If Julia was slightly more knowledgeable about Judaism she could articulate her point in a scholarly manner, saying: 'While Judaism remains unchanged, you can still be Jewish without being a religious Jew.' Judaism and Jewish-ness are different categories. While Judaism is an unchanged religious core, Jewish-ness is a dynamic category in a continuous flux. Indeed, this is the case with Zionism. Zionism is a dynamic continuation of Jewish-ness: it is racist, exclusive, supremacist and self-centred, yet it is not Judaic. It has very little to do with Judaism. It may be messianic in a territorial sense, yet it lacks the Judaic divinity. In fact, in this sense, Zionism opposes Judaism.

47. Alan Dershowitz (born September 1, 1938) is an American lawyer, jurist, and political commentator. Dershowitz is an outspoken supporter of Israel. In 2003 he published The Case for Israel, an advocacy of the Zionist cause and Israeli policies. In March 2006, Mearsheimer and Walt, the authors of The Israel Lobby and U.S. Foreign Policy (The London Review of Books) referred to Dershowitz specifically as an 'apologist' for the Israel lobby.

48. Max Nordau, speech at the First Zionist Congress, Basel, Switzerland, 29 August 1897. See http://www.jewishvirtualli-

brary.org/jsource/Zionism/nordau1.html [accessed 15/06/2010].

49. Avnery, Uri, 'I'm a Leftist, but ...', *Counterpunch*, 8 September 2006; see www.counterpunch.org/avnery09082006.html

50. Ibid

51. A Tel Aviv University poll that took place at the time of the Israeli military campaign in Gaza (2008-2009) revealed that IDF's operation against Hamas in Gaza enjoyed the overwhelming support of Israeli Jews, despite the loss of civilian life. A whopping 94% of the Israeli Jewish population supported or strongly supported the operation, while 92% thought it beneficial to Israel's security. The poll found that 92% of Israeli Jews thought the air force's attacks in Gaza justified, despite the suffering of the civilian population in the Strip and the damage they cause to infrastructure. http://www.jpost.com/Home/Article.aspx?id=129307

52. http://www.israelnationalnews.com/News/News.aspx/124345

53. Weininger, Otto, *Sex and Character*, New York: Howard Fertig, 2003, p. 29.

54. Ibid, p. 57.

55. Ibid, p. 110.

56. Ibid, Preface, p. I.

57. Ibid, p. 109.

58. Ibid, p. 304.

59. Ibid, p. 305.

60. Marx, Karl, 'On the Jewish Question' ('*Zur Judenfrage*'), first published in February 1844 in *Deutsch-Französische Jahrbücher*; see translation at http://www.marxists.org/archive/marx/works/1844/jewish-question/

61. Weininger, Otto, *Sex and Character*, New York: Howard Fertig, 2003

62. Shavit, Ari, 'Leaving the Zionist Ghetto', interview with Avraham Burg, *Ha'aretz*, 25 July 2007; accessed 15/06/2010 at http://peacepalestine.blogspot.com/2007/06/complete-

abraham-burg-interview-leaving.html

63. *Aliyah* is the Hebrew word describing the immigration of Jews to *Eretz Yisrael*. It is a basic tenet of Zionist ideology. *Aliyah* means 'ascent'. The opposite action i.e. emigration of Jews from Israel, is referred to as *yerida* (descent).

64. Speech on the Place of the Bund in the R.S.D.L.P, V. I. Lenin, July 17 (30)-August 10 (23), 1903

65. See http://www.matzpen.org/index.asp?p=principles

66. http://www.thefreemanonline.org/columns/capitalism-and-the-jews/

67. http://www.law.uchicago.edu/audio/friedman101578

68. http://classiques.uqac.ca/classiques/sombart_werner/Jews _and_modern_capitalism/sombart_jews_capitalism.pdf

69. 'What is the secular basis of Judaism? *Practical* need, *self-interest*. What is the worldly religion of the Jew? *Huckstering.* What is his worldly God? *Money.* Very well then! Emancipation from huckstering and money, consequently from practical, real Judaism, would be the self-emancipation of our time.' Karl Marx *On The Jewish Question*, 1844

70. Defined earlier on as a second category.

71. Falls into the third category.

72. This is to suggest that the liberation from despots and oppressive systems, must be always primarily grounded on ethical foundation.

73. Right-wing Israeli journalist Yair Sheleg in *Ha'aretz*, 2006 see http://www.haaretz.com/hasen/spages/757767.html

74. Rappaport, Meron, 'IDF commander: We fired more than a million cluster bombs in Lebanon', *Ha'aretz*, 12 September 2006; see http://www.haaretz.com/hasen/spages/761781.html

75. On 31 May 2010, in international waters, Israeli Navy seals raided a humanitarian aid flotilla of six ships. The flotilla carried humanitarian aid and construction materials. It aimed to break the Israeli siege on Gaza. At dawn, hundreds of Israeli elite Shayetet 13 naval commandos boarded the ships

from speedboats and helicopters, using excessive power. On the Turkish MV Mavi Marmara, the Israelis met some resistance. The Israelis were quick to use live ammunition. Consequently, nine Turkish peace activists were killed by the Israeli soldiers, some amongst them were executed by Israeli soldiers. The Israeli raid led to widespread international condemnation.

76. The Invention of the Jewish People, Shlomo Sand, Verso 2009, pg 1.

77. Ilani, Ofri, 'Shattering a "National Mythology"', interview with Shlomo Sand, *Ha'aretz*, 21 March 2008; see http://www.haaretz.com/general/shattering-a-national-mythology-1.242015

78. The Invention of the Jewish People, Shlomo Sand, Verso 2009, pg 21

79. The Invention of the Jewish People, Shlomo Sand, Verso 2009, pg 66

80. Ilani, Ofri, 'Shattering a "National Mythology"', interview with Shlomo Sand, *Ha'aretz*, 21 March 2008; see http://www.haaretz.com/general/shattering-a-national-mythology-1.242015

81. Ilani, Ofri, 'Shattering a "National Mythology"', interview with Shlomo Sand, *Ha'aretz*, 21 March 2008; see http://www.haaretz.com/general/shattering-a-national-mythology-1.242015

82. Ibid

83. Ibid

84. Ilani, 'Shattering a "National Mythology"'

85. Berbers are the indigenous peoples of North Africa west of the Nile Valley

86. Ibid.

87. Ibid.

88. Ibid.

89. AIPAC – The American Israel Public Affairs Committee is the

leading Israeli lobbying group in the USA. It advocates pro-Israel policies within American politics and other influential institutions.

The New York Times described AIPAC as 'the most important organisation affecting America's relationship with Israel.' It is no doubt one of the most powerful lobbying groups in Washington, DC, and its critics have stated it acts as an agent of the Israeli government, with a 'stranglehold' on the United States Congress.

Along its history AIPAC has been caught in a few espionage affairs. In 2005, a Pentagon analyst pleaded guilty to charges of passing US government secrets to two AIPAC staffers in what is known as the AIPAC espionage scandal.

In 1984 the FBI investigated after Israeli Minister of Economics Dan Halpern passed stolen classified US government documents to AIPAC, outlining trade secrets of major US industries lobbying against the US-Israel Free Trade Area.

90. http://www.gush-shalom.org/archives/article348.html

91. http://www.tikkun.org/article.php/20090617074540771

92. 30. Ellis, Marc H., *Beyond Innocence and Redemption: Confronting The Holocaust and Israeli Power: Creating a Moral Future for the Jewish People*, San Francisco, Harper & Row, 1990, p. ???

93. Bowman, Glenn, 'Migrant Labour: Constructing Homeland in the Exilic Imagination', *Anthropological Theory* II:4, December 2002, pp. 447–68.

94. Lemche, Niels Peter, The Canaanites and Their Land, Sheffield: Sheffield Academic Press, 1991.

95. Ibid

96. Medoff, Rafael, 'A Purim Lesson: Lobbying Against Genocide, Then and Now'; see http://www.wymaninstitute.org/articles /2004-03-purim.php

97. Ibid

98. Ibid

99. Ibid

100. Ibid

101. Prinz, Joachim, *Zionism under the Nazi Government, Young Zionist* (London, November 1937), p.18; cited in Brenner, Lenni, *Zionism in the Age of the Dictators*, Westport, CT: Lawrence Hill & Co., 1983; see http://www.marxists.de/middleast/brenner /ch05.htm

102. Cited in Brenner, *ibid*.

103. Brenner, *ibid*.

104. Strauss, Herbert (ed.), *Gegenwart Im Ruckblick* (Heidelberg, 1970), p.231; cited at http://www.marxists.de/middleast /brenner/ch03.htm#n1

105. Brenner, Lenni, interview with Joachim Prinz, 8 February 1981; see http://cosmos.ucc.ie/cs1064/jabowen/IPSC/php /clip.php ?cid=512

106. Littlewood, Stuart, 'Jews are eight times over-represented in UK parliament', 21 May 2010; see http://www.redress.cc/global /slittlewood20100521

107. Bruck, Connie, 'The Influencer', *The New Yorker*, 10 May 2010.

108. http://www.ynetnews.com/articles/0,7340,L-3624394,00.html

109. http://www.thejc.com/news/uk-news/26593/war-crimes-will-government-ever-act

110. Zionism was, in fact, the only Jewish secular ideology to come close to something that resembles an autonomous and authentic body of Jewish secular moral thinking. As discussed before, Zionism promised to bring about a civilized and ethical Jew.

Index

Contemporary culture has eliminated both the concept of the public and the figure of the intellectual. Former public spaces – both physical and cultural – are now either derelict or colonized by advertising. A cretinous anti-intellectualism presides, cheerled by expensively educated hacks in the pay of multinational corporations who reassure their bored readers that there is no need to rouse themselves from their interpassive stupor. The informal censorship internalized and propagated by the cultural workers of late capitalism generates a banal conformity that the propaganda chiefs of Stalinism could only ever have dreamt of imposing. Zer0 Books knows that another kind of discourse – intellectual without being academic, popular without being populist – is not only possible: it is already flourishing, in the regions beyond the striplit malls of so-called mass media and the neurotically bureaucratic halls of the academy. Zer0 is committed to the idea of publishing as a making public of the intellectual. It is convinced that in the unthinking, blandly consensual culture in which we live, critical and engaged theoretical reflection is more important than ever before.